/20

Poetry and the Child

Poetry and the Child

FORMERLY TITLED 'POETRY IN THE ELEMENTARY CLASSROOM'

FLORA J. ARNSTEIN

DOVER PUBLICATIONS, INC.
NEW YORK

Published in Canada by General Publishing Company, Ltd., 30 Lesmill Road, Don Mills, Toronto,
Ontario.
Published in the United Kingdom by Constable
and Company, Ltd., 10 Orange Street, London WC 2.

This Dover edition, first published in 1970, is an
unabridged and slightly corrected republication of
the work originally published by Appleton-Century-
Crofts, a Division of Meredith Publishing Company,
New York, in 1962 under the title *Poetry in the
Elementary Classroom*. The 1962 edition was a pub-
lication of The National Council of Teachers of
English.

International Standard Book Number: 0-486-21663-2
Library of Congress Catalog Card Number: 79-133270

Manufactured in the United States of America
Dover Publications, Inc.
180 Varick Street
New York, N.Y. 10014

FOREWORD

THE ONLY TRUE POETS are children, someone has said. Their fascination with language, their "built-in" ability to use it in unique and original ways, their skill in making language work for them in conveying their experiences and their thoughts are most pronounced among the very young. This is true because only the young child has not lived long enough to be influenced in his use of language by adults. Very early in life well-meaning adults often shape and bind the child's naturally poetic use of language into stilted, conforming, "correct" speech. Teachers are the most vulnerable on this score.

The three-year-old, resting for a moment in the play area on a New York nursery school roof, explained to her teacher that she was being "quiet as smoke." Here is truly poetic language. Any parent or teacher of the threes to sixes can match this illustration with equally potent expressions of the creative use of language by children.

The young child's zest for and skill in using language creatively must be fostered as he grows toward maturity. Mrs. Arnstein's *Poetry and the Child* becomes for the sensitive teacher, and hopefully for the sensitive parent, a tool which can make poetry a living force in the development of children.

If poetry is to make a difference in the lives of children, we must look at the teacher and the goals he has for his children. Next to parents, the teacher frequently exerts the greatest influence in the life of a child.

A good teacher is primarily concerned with the full flowering of personality. He knows the "ingredients" necessary for personality development:

—a climate which fosters freedom to explore, discover, and dream

—opportunities to share emotions, thoughts, and ideas

—skills which conserve rather than squander the creative powers of children.

v

A good teacher believes that poetry encompasses the "ingredients" necessary for the fruition of personality. He not only believes this; he communicates it to children in many ways:

—Through awareness of the beauty and power of words. His appreciation of words is as deep as that of the child in Mary Ellen Chase's delightful bit of autobiography, *The White Gate,* who upon being given a tiny safe for her choice possessions, kept within the depository pink slips of paper upon which were written favorite words. These were taken out from time to time and savored. The good teacher will help children discover their own unique ways of collecting words which have meaning for the collectors. Rich and frequent experience with poetry will stimulate word collectors to greater effort.

—Through recognizing that feelings are as potent as facts; that feelings *are* facts. And in no aspect of the curriculum is there as rich a source of "feelings" as in poetry. The teacher of tens to eighteens, concerned with developing concepts of the American heritage, may cram all of the knowledge he possesses into the minds of his social studies students, but unless these youngsters get the "feel" of those who helped establish a great nation, information soon departs. The good teacher will make sure that the great poetry of the American heritage is as much in the consciousness of his youngsters' experience as is the history of our nation. He will read appropriate passages from Benét's *Western Star,* for example, where children living in the present period of social revolution will find reflected the past tradition of "man's inhumanity to man." They will find within the beauty of Benét's great narrative poem the hostility of old New Castle and feel with the stranger as the inhabitants "whip the first Quaker bloodily through the streets."

—Through stimulating children to find in the commonplace a spur to the imagination. Only a teacher who is alert to the magic in the first snowfall of the season or the eeriness of thick fog will find the opportunities to make the world of reality and the world of the imagination one world for the child. Herein are opportunities for helping children become sensitive to the fact that poets express their own experiences in ways that are distinctly unique. "Fog" is the title of equally delightful poems by Sandburg, Farjeon, and Rossetti; each is different; yet each tells us as much about the subject.

In this book the author shows how teachers may work creatively with the individual child or with children in small groups and in large classes. For teachers eager to enrich their own content resources as well as their skills in conveying to children the "use value" of poetry in their lives, Mrs. Arnstein has provided an instrument of great value. Of greater value, *Poetry and the Child* has the potential for bringing to fruition the poet that is in every child.

MURIEL CROSBY

Wilmington Public Schools
Wilmington, Delaware

PREFACE

THE IDEA FOR THIS BOOK suggested itself to me after a talk I gave to a gathering of teachers. I became aware that during the "question-and-answer" period the identical questions were posed whenever I spoke to teacher groups: How do you get children interested in poetry? How do you get them to write? What can a teacher do on being required to teach poetry when he feels his background in the subject inadequate? It occurred to me that perhaps a book dealing with their common problems might be of service to teachers and help to provide them with confidence in their ability to handle the teaching of poetry.

But more than this, I felt that such a book might give the needed assurance that poetry by its nature is not antipathetic to children, as is generally supposed; also that it is not forbidding to teach. Through examples of poetry written by children, by quotations from their own comments I hoped it would be demonstrated that children bring to the study of poetry an eager and lively interest; likewise, as the result of this interest and through their engagement with writing, that children achieve a notably enhanced awareness and appreciation of poetry which may serve as a firm foundation for future poetry study.

So in the hope that not only the children might prosper through my sharing the fruits of my experience, but that teachers themselves might derive new-found pleasure in poetry and fresh encouragement and incentive to teach it, this book was undertaken.

F.J.A.

CONTENTS

Poetry and the Child

1

Why Poetry?

THE PASTURE

I'm going out to clean the pasture spring;
I'll only stop to rake the leaves away
(And wait to watch the water clear, I may):
I shan't be gone long.—You come too.

I'm going out to fetch the little calf
That's standing by the mother. It's so young
It totters when she licks it with her tongue.
I shan't be gone long.—You come too.[1]

HERE IS A POEM by Robert Frost, one of the great poets of today. It is a poem accessible to everyone. There is no word in it that is not comprehensible to any eight-year-old. It is simple in syntax and in meaning —even the below-the-surface meaning that older children are quick to discern. And it is poetry—that bugbear which many readers and teachers claim they cannot understand, much less enjoy.

What has produced this widespread distaste for poetry? Poetry is an art, as are music and painting, and as such it is intended for our enjoyment. There are, of course, a few tone-deaf people, or some unresponsive to the graphic arts. But by and large people enjoy listening to music and viewing paintings, as is attested to by the numbers who attend concerts and visit galleries. Why, then, is poetry alone of the arts so neglected?

For many teachers it presents a bewildering subject. They recognize that something about the teaching of poetry differs from the teaching of social science, arithmetic, or even English in general. They feel ill at

---

[1] From Robert Frost, *Complete Poems of Robert Frost* (New York: Holt, Rinehart and Winston, 1949). Originally in *North of Boston* (Holt).

ease when called upon to teach even the token amount of poetry included in most English courses. They are not to be blamed for their bewilderment. They themselves are the product of teachers who have shared their own lack of preparation. The poetry to which each group was exposed in its youth seemed as meaningless, as devoid of value as today's teachers suspect will be the poems they are called upon to present to their own pupils. How this vicious circle can be broken, how poetry can become meaningful to children will be the burden of this book.

We shall have to begin by revising our own concepts of poetry. Many of us are responsive to music and art; yet the aesthetic response to poetry is as available to us as that of the other arts if we are able to approach it in an amenable spirit. That we feel ourselves unable to do so is mainly the result of two deterrents: 1, the manner in which poetry was presented to us in our youth, and 2, the idea that poetry is something remote, esoteric. Let us deal with the last mentioned first.

We have already noted that in "The Pasture" there is nothing, even at a first reading, that is not readily understandable. It deals with an *experience* on a farm—the farmer going out in an early month of the year to clean a spring that has become clogged with the winter's debris. He is also planning to bring into shelter a newborn calf. Regarded at this level, the poem presents simply an experience which must be a common one for farmers, but which is not beyond the imaginative grasp of city people. Boiled down to its essence it is merely a reconstruction of an experience. And, here is the point, all poetry is just that: the presentation in words of experience either actual or imagined. Of course it goes without saying that poetry is something more than that as well; we shall explore the "more" as we proceed. But for the moment let us be concerned with poetry as recorded experience.

Even the youngest child is constantly involved in experiencing. Before he can speak he is feeling and either consciously or unconsciously recording and remembering experience. So here is something that we may build on—the child's own experience, the most necessary adjunct to his growth, indeed to his living. What we have to do is to relate his experience to that of other people and, in the matter of poetry, to that of the poet. Let us take, for example, the experience of climbing a hill. We might talk with the children about the various aspects of climbing a hill, of looking down, of noting what things look like from this vantage point, and we might invite the children to relate their own experiences of hill-climb-ing. After each has had the opportunity to make his contribution to the subject, the teacher might say, "Here is what one poet felt and thought about going up a hill." Then she might read them "Afternoon on a Hill" by Edna St. Vincent Millay.

> I will be the gladdest thing
>   Under the sun!
> I will touch a hundred flowers
>   And not pick one.
>
> I will look at cliffs and clouds
>   With quiet eyes,
> Watch the wind bow down the grass,
>   And the grass rise.
>
> And when lights begin to show
>   Up from the town,
> I will mark which must be mine,
>   And then start down![2]

Through the children's recalling and relating their own experiences, they have built a bridge between themselves and the poet; it has been brought home to them, not in so many words, of course, that poetry deals with experience and that experience is a two-way road that may be shared with poets.

The concept of poetry as experience and the invitation to children to relive their own experiences serve to rob poetry of that remoteness that bedevils our usual attitude toward it. Unless children are conditioned unfavorably to poetry, they are not inclined to feel this remoteness. And if the teacher evaluates his own experience, examining it in the light of what it has brought to him in his own life, he too may begin to feel at home in the world of poetry. No one is so insensitive that he has not at some time been awed by the power of waves crashing on rocky shores, or has not been moved by the silence and majesty of a moonlit night. Bringing back to mind our own reactions at such times, we can reacti-vate our sensitivity to the less spectacular but no less meaningful day-

[2] From Edna St. Vincent Millay, *Collected Poems* (New York: Harper & Row, 1956).

to-day experiences. This recalling may in turn make us more aware of the child's constant experiencing. We may then become more sympathetic to and more understanding of his thoughts and feelings regarding those matters which touch upon his daily life.

By giving respectful attention to his genuine reactions we can hope to lead him toward values of more significance than some of those offered him in our present culture. Many movies that children are exposed to are designed mainly for adult consumption, and the subject matter dealt with as well as the frequent depiction of violence is hardly conducive to the children's developing a response to the more meaningful values our culture is heir to. The same may be said of advertising with its stress on material possessions. If we permit rock and roll to replace all other music, the "quick draw" to supplant sounder dramatic presentations, the possession of "the latest" in clothes and gadgets to take precedence over everything else, we rob the child of the ability to relate to the significant features in our culture; we close down to him the opportunity to enjoy the great music, the art, the poetry that the past makes available.

What can be offered our children to counteract the merely sensational which tends to deaden response to all less titillating offerings? It may seem fantastic to suggest as antidote the quiet, seemingly unexciting adventure into poetry. To anticipate the skepticism that such a suggestion will arouse is not difficult. How can poetry compete with the suspense of a movie, a jazz session, a ride in a speeding car? Well, let us admit from the start that we are not speaking of competition. We speak of something on quite another plane. The case for poetry rests on what this plane has to offer that no other aspect of our culture does to today's children.

What is it, let us first ask, that children today are deprived of? Is it not the opportunity to experience life in a deeper sense than the superficiality, the speed of today's living makes possible? Are not children too often deprived of experience at first hand—or if not that, then are they not exposed to experiences following so closely, one upon the heels of the other, that there is no time to absorb, to assess, to do more than skim the surface of any single one? Against this superficiality, poetry allows a child a certain perspective, allows him to stand off from his own experience, to recall it, to relate it to the experience of others, and by so doing to accord the experience a value that it would not otherwise have for him. And this value takes on greater dimensions as the child realizes the significance that adults and, in this special case, poets place upon it. The wealth and scope of poetry offer children a wide range for thoughtful consideration. What other subject matter can draw upon so extensive a field, and what other can touch so closely each person's private store?

It is this personal relation to poetry and the satisfaction such a relation entails that is responsible, I believe, for the continued interest of the children I have taught. In a lifetime of teaching I have found group after group responding happily to the poetry sessions. Much of the children's satisfaction derives from their own writing, from the tapping of their creative resources; this aspect will be dealt with later. But that the reading and discussion of the matter of poetry, the opportunity offered children to explore, to formulate their own thoughts and feelings —that all this is meaningful to them has been proved to me beyond a doubt. What is in question here is not alone satisfaction and enjoyment; it is a deeper realization of life, a fuller appreciation of the world around us, a more sensitive ability to identify with others, in effect, a capacity to bring to living something more than a cursory glimpse in passing.

In addition the discussing and airing of ordinarily repressed thoughts and feelings affords the child a therapeutic outlet. Visitors to our classes have commented upon the relaxation attendant upon the poetry sessions. Also the poems of some of the children have attested to a release of tension and pressure. One girl says, "Sometimes when I am troubled, I feel the most like writing," and in illustration she writes:

> It's funny that sometimes when I'm most quiet and peaceful
> It is hardest to write poems.
> Sometimes when it's noisy,
> And I am disturbed in my mind,
> Poems come quite easily.[3]

Many restless children have become calmer during the hour devoted to poetry and, surprisingly, many children say "thank you" on departing from class.

In contrast to the approach to poetry that I have outlined is that to which we were subjected in our youth. I might guess that my own

[3] From Flora J. Arnstein, *Children Write Poetry: A Creative Approach* (New York: Dover Publications, Inc., 1967; originally published as *Adventures into Poetry*, Stanford University Press, 1951).

experience was fairly typical. In my preteens I was required to memorize "Thanatopsis" by William Cullen Bryant, a poem whose subject is death, and, it must be admitted, death treated in rather a grisly fashion:

> When thoughts
> Of the last bitter hour come like a blight
> Over thy spirit, and sad images
> Of the stern agony, and shroud, and pall,
> And breathless darkness, and the narrow house,
> Make thee to shudder, and grow sick at heart . . .

Also I was required to memorize lines from Milton's "L'Allegro." Now neither of these poems is in any way appropriate for children. The first, both in vocabulary and concept, is not within the range of a child's experience. The philosophic exhortation to resort to nature "when thoughts of the last hour" beset us has little to offer to a child; actually all I brought away from it was a sense of horror that it required years to efface. The second, beginning

> Hence, loathèd Melancholy,
> Of Cerberus and blackest Midnight born . . .

deals in its opening lines with a state of mind that is, hopefully, not related to a child. The entire poem is so stylized and so alien in vocabulary as to make the memorizing of it a dread chore. Such memorization imposes upon many children a real hardship that is responsible, I believe, along with remote subject matter and forbidding vocabulary, for the frequent distaste of children for poetry. I might interpolate here that I have never required memorizing of my children—I have avoided it as I have any other task that might seem onerous, since my object has always been to make the poetry experience a pleasurable one.

Some of the more accessible poems offered children I believe to be equally inappropriate for them. "The Village Blacksmith" and many others of the sort have a sentimental aura unacceptable to today's children,[4] and the didactic poems particularly are not calculated to

---

[4] One twelve-year-old girl, a member of one of my out-of-school classes, reported: "We had the most horrible poem in school today," and then she grimaced and in a mincing voice recited: "Blessings on thee, little man,/Barefoot boy with cheek of tan."

contribute to a love of poetry. Is it any wonder, considering what we were offered in the name of poetry, that when the school demands were over we should never turn to poetry in the hope of any pleasure to be derived from it? If we, as teachers, try to efface these early memories, we can then approach poetry with an open mind and enjoy what poets have to tell us that is relevant to our lives today. Only then can we bring to children our newly discovered pleasure in poetry and invite them to share with us what it offers.

2

The Teacher's Dilemma

ONE OF THE MOST FREQUENT questions teachers ask me is, "How can one teach poetry when one has insufficient background in it oneself?" Understandably this situation seems almost impossible to resolve. Teachers know only too well that they will be unable to instill in their pupils an interest in poetry if they possess none themselves. The answer is there is no immutable law requiring that they continue without interest in poetry. Here is a field that will be enriching for personal reasons as well as for teaching. And what if, in the exploring, teachers are only one jump ahead of their pupils? Jumping is fun and the imminence of having one's heels trod on is a prime incentive to effort on one's own part.

The first step might be to secure an anthology of modern poetry—perhaps not the latest anthology, since it must be admitted that some modern poetry (just as some modern art and music) is difficult to understand. But many paperbacks are readily available—notably anthologies by Oscar Williams[1]—that contain a wealth of poetry that is readily grasped.

Guides to one's first faltering footsteps are the very readable books of Babette Deutsch and Elizabeth Drew. The latter has recently issued, under the imprint of the Dell Laurel Poetry Series, a book entitled *Poetry: A Modern Guide to Its Understanding and Enjoyment*, which is to be recommended most highly.[2] If the teacher is primarily interested in the creative approach to poetry, there are the invaluable volumes of Hughes Mearns, a pioneer in creative work with children: *Creative*

[1] E.g., Oscar Williams (editor), *The New Pocket Anthology of American Verse* (New York: Washington Square Press, 1961) and *Pocket Book of Modern Verse* (New York: Washington Square Press, 1960).

[2] The National Council of Teachers of English has compiled a bibliography of Critical Anthologies for the Teacher and a list of Collections of Standard Verse.

Youth[3] and *The Creative Adult*.[4] The first gives a picture of a school environment which sets free the creative spirit. It contains stories about the children, their conversations, and along with these the author's illuminating commentary on the means for kindling and encouraging the writing of poetry. *The Creative Adult* is not specifically addressed to teachers but contains much valuable material and a heartening encouragement to experiment. An excellent book, unfortunately out of print, but possibly available in some libraries, is *Enjoying Poetry in School* by Howard Francis Seely.[5]

But the main suggestion is that the teacher read poetry, that he forget any obligation to "appreciate" or indulge in any critical appraisal. Appreciation grows with exposure to poetry as one's own preference and taste develop. To plunge in, to get the "feel" of poetry as something to be savored—that is all that is necessary for a start; this, and for the teacher to rid himself of two holdovers from his early conception of poetry: the idea that poetry must "teach a lesson" and that it has to do with sentiment. Poetry does deal with emotion, but the sentiment which is popularly associated with it from the past is more likely to be sentimentality. The gap between sentiment and sentimentality is a great one, though the distinction for the beginning poetry reader may be difficult to make. We all tend to accept conventional "sentiment," so that we fall into the trap of the easy and familiar. But by enlarging our vision, putting it to the test of the genuine in emotion—emotion that is truly felt and rooted in reality—we need no longer be beguiled by the facile, the trite. However, the new poetry reader need not worry. Taste and discrimination grow as one reads, and the teacher may be guided by the poems in anthologies collected by acclaimed and established poets. Let him select poems that appeal to him and reread these to find how much a poem has to give beyond its first impact.

Turning again to "The Pasture," which, as printed in Robert Frost's volume *North of Boston* appears in italics before the table of contents, the teacher might ask himself, and later his children, why the poet chose to place the poem where he did instead of in the body of the

---

[3] (New York: Dover Publications, 1959).
[4] (New York: Doubleday, 1940).
[5] (Richmond, Va.: Johnson Publishing, 1931). My book *Children Write Poetry*, while containing some material included in this present book, goes into greater detail regarding the children's poetry and deals with other matter that will not be herein included.

book. The children answer the question with one of their own: "Was Frost intending the invitation to the pasture as an invitation to the poetry?" Also he might ask why (aside from the rhyme) does the poet say that the little calf "totters when she licks it with her tongue," instead of something to the effect that it was unsteady on its feet? The children are quick to discover that the last is merely a flat statement, whereas the phrase "tottering when she licks it with her tongue" gives a vivid picture of the precarious stance of the little calf far better than an explanatory phrase could do. This picture-making quality of poetry is illustrated in the following poem by Sara Tearsdale:

FULL MOON
(Santa Barbara)

I listened. There was not a sound to hear
  In the great rain of moonlight pouring down,
The eucalpytus trees were carved in silver,
  And a light mist of silver lulled the town.
I saw far off the gray Pacific bearing
  A broad white disk of flame,
And on the garden-walk a snail beside me
  Tracing in crystal the slow way he came.[6]

Here the moonlight "pours down" in a "great rain"; the eucalyptus is "carved in silver"; and notably we have the snail "tracing in crystal the slow way he came." I venture to say no child after reading this will ever look at a snail's trail as he has before—the crystal tracing will have become part of his mental baggage.

Joseph Conrad in his preface to *The Nigger of the Narcissus* expresses the credo of a great artist. He says: "My task which I am trying to achieve is, by the power of the written word, to make you hear, to make you feel—that is, before all to make you *see*. That—and no more, and it is everything." Robert Browning in his poem "Fra Lippo Lippi" has his painter say:

> For, don't you mark, we're made so that we love
> First when we see them painted, things we have passed
> Perhaps a hundred times nor cared to see;
>
> . . . .
>
> Art was given us for that.

[6] From Sara Teasdale, *Dark of the Moon* (New York: Macmillan, 1926).

Matthew Arnold assigns to poetry the "power of so dealing with things as to awaken in us a wonderful, new and intimate sense of them and our relation to them."

All these artists, the prose writer, the painter, the poet, are asking their readers and viewers to see with the inner eye, with the imagination, and by doing so to re-create for themselves the emotion that gave rise to the work of art. This re-creation of the emotion is one of the essential objects of poetry. For poetry is not a purely intellectual fabrication. It has its roots in the feeling world—all the way from the tactile sensations, the auditory, the visual, to the most complex feelings arising from our most subtle, deeply felt emotions. The poet John Ciardi says, "A poet thinks with his senses, his nerve endings, his whole body . . . He *feels* what he thinks."[7] And this is primarily the way children think.

The sensory aspect of poetry is particularly related to children, for their senses are not yet jaded and respond eagerly to experience which is still to them delightfully fresh and new. Fay, eight years old, writes:

> I love to work in clay
> And get my hands all sticky
> And then I squeeze it,
> And then it gets all dry,
> And then I can't work with it
> Because it crumbles up.[8]

Sylvia, seven, dictates:

> I love to hear the sea roaring,
> And then go wading,
> And then come out
> And watch the little bugs
> Crawl along the sand,
> And then pick up shells.
> Oh, how I love to hear the sea roaring.

Alan, ten, writes:

SWIMMING

> I love to feel water's icy fingers
> (That wrap me like a blanket)
> Grasping me.

[7] *Saturday Review* (November 22, 1958).

[8] From Flora J. Arnstein, *Children Write Poetry* (New York: Dover Publications, Inc., 1967).

Ruth, eleven, writes:

> The sand is yellow golden,
> But when you dig down deeper,
> It becomes a darker brown.
> The water is blue with white foam,
> With shells down in the bottom.
> Sometimes the shells are washed up on the shore,
> But when I see them
> They are all smashed and crushed.
> You can see jelly-fish down by the shore, too,
> The sky is a lovely deep blue
> With a great big enormous round sun.

These and countless more of the children's poems describe in exact terms their sense impressions—feeling, hearing, seeing.

When the teacher comes to read poetry with the children, he need not be surprised that there already exists in them a bond with poetry. No barrier blocks their direct response, and, in some inexplicable way, this response induces an interplay between him and the children that provides for him an unanticipated pleasure in the poetry he is sharing with them. Sharing is the key word. Let the teacher forget he is teaching poetry; let him rather share it and together with the children discover and enjoy what it has to offer. The more he is able to derive enjoyment himself, the more will the children do likewise, for nothing is so contagious as enthusiasm, provided that it is genuine and not forced.

As to the teaching of a lesson, previously referred to, while our literature contains many didactic poems, most people, and especially children, do not savor being preached at. It might be better to allow poetry of this nature to go by the board. In addition, in some didactic poetry the lesson takes precedence over the poetry, which is an added reason to eschew it, since it is the poetry with which we are primarily concerned. Poetry should not be made the vehicle for moral instruction —that is, if it is to minister to enjoyment, nor should the poetry session be the occasion for moral pronouncements upon what the children say. Discussion, if it is to have any value, can result only if the children feel free to talk spontaneously.

Another aspect of poetry that the novice reader may enjoy is the connotative as against the denotative function of words. To simplify—

denotative words are those essential to science and to informative writing. They are the words that are most exact, that strictly delimit meaning in order to pinpoint fact. Connotative words are valuable to poetry. They are the words that have accrued to themselves a wealth of meanings, overtones of feeling, latitudes that stimulate the imagination. John Ciardi says in the article previously quoted: "A word [in poetry] has far more meaning . . . than in factual prose. A word is not a meaning but a complex of meanings consisting of all its possibilities: its ability to identify something, the images it releases in making that identification, its sound, its history, its association in context with other words of the passage. Good poets use *more* of a word than most readers are used to."

Robert Frost has been quoted as saying that poetry is that which escapes in translation, which in effect means that the words of poetry have for those who speak the same language an aura of meaning, of feeling, of allusion that cannot be exactly duplicated in a foreign language. For words are an integral part of the culture of a people and evoke in the reader memories and associations that are not necessarily shared by readers of an alien culture. The poet avails himself of just this evocative power inherent in words so that his readers may approximate his own feelings in relation to the matter that concerns him at the moment.

Let us look at the following poem by Alice Meynell for pertinent illustration.

THE SHEPHERDESS

She walks—the lady of my delight—
    A shepherdess of sheep.
Her flocks are thoughts. She keeps them white;
    She guards them from the steep;
She feeds them on the fragrant height,
    And folds them in for sleep.

She roams maternal hills and bright,
    Dark valleys safe and deep.
Into that tender breast at night
    The chastest stars may peep.
She walks—the lady of my delight—
    A shepherdess of sheep.

> She holds her little thoughts in sight.
> Though gay they run and leap.
> She is so circumspect and right;
> She has her soul to keep.
> She walks—the lady of my delight—
> A shepherdess of sheep.[9]

This poem, selected almost at random, contains words that most happily illustrate what is meant by connotation. Take the word "fragrant," which might stir our remembrance of perhaps gardens at night, of the warm scent of newly ripened fruit; a host of other associations might come to mind, so that the "fragrant height" becomes something that is not a description of height, but of height trailing lovely odors rarefied in the upper air. So too the "maternal" hills, in which maternal has no precise meaning as applied to hills, but carries the connotation of something warm and protective, which concept is reinforced by the "valleys safe and deep." Neither adjective, "fragrant" or "maternal," is used literally, yet how much more dynamic and effective each is than literal, descriptive words would be.

If this stressing of the value of connotative words seems to contradict the earlier example of the "tottering" calf, it is just to make the point that poetry includes both the most happily chosen exact words to paint specific pictures and the most suggestive evocative words to arouse appropriate emotions. Also, in some instances, a word may be at the same time denotative and connotative, as in a sense "tottering" is. This encompassing scope of language in poetry may be the source of continuous aesthetic enjoyment. The reader arrives at a sense of discovery when he finds shopworn words revitalized by use in a fresh context, and he finds himself rejecting the clichés that are so prevalent in sentimental poetry.

One way in which poets use what John Ciardi calls "more of a word" is notable in the following poem by James Joyce.

NOISE OF WATERS

> All day I hear the noise of waters
> Making moan,

[9] From Alice Meynell, *The Poems of Alice Meynell* (New York: Scribner's, 1923).

Sad as the sea-bird is, when going
        Forth alone,
He hears the winds cry to the waters'
        Monotone.

The grey winds, the cold winds are blowing
        Where I go.
I hear the noise of many waters
        Far below.
All day, all night, I hear them flowing
        To and fro.[10]

Observe how the poet's choice of words with long "O" sounds—*moan, alone, monotone, go, below, fro*—contributes to the mood of melancholy. The new readers of poetry will discover many instances of this relation of the sound of words to mood. They will note, too, the use of onomatopoeia—that jawbreaking word which means simply the use of words that imitate or illustrate natural sounds, such as *crack, break, tinkle*. At the appropriate time the teacher may initiate the children into this magic power of words; he will find them eagerly responsive and avid to make their own discoveries.

Imagery, which plays such a large role in poetry, is another aspect that may engage the new reader. Describing one object in terms of another is such a common practice that we do not realize we are making use of imagery when we say, "He was quiet as a church mouse," or something is "as cold as ice." In poetry the juxtaposition of two disparate objects by reference to a characteristic that is shared by both is a deliberate device. In some strange way the very difference of the two objects compared seems to add to the impact of the image, to add another dimension to the description.

In "The Shepherdess," quoted earlier, the entire poem is an image. The lover likens his lady to a shepherdess—her thoughts are flocks—and he sustains this image throughout the poem. But there need not be such continuity. In "Full Moon" we have the images of moonlight compared to rain and the snail's trail to a tracing of silver. We may, then, expect to find in poetry much expression that is not literal; rather, the play of imagination makes use of words for their power of sugges-

[10] From James Joyce, "Chamber Music," Stanza XXV, in *Collected Poems* (New York: Viking, 1937).

tion, for their power to arouse emotion, and for their ability to make us contribute our own imaginative identification with the poet and what he is saying.

Children are very receptive to images, although, needless to say, this would not be true of very young children. Also they are frequently surprised to find that they have made spontaneous use of images in poems of their own writing. Image-making is natural to all people, children as well as adults: one little girl in an elevator asked me, "What shelf do we get off at?" and my little grandson once remarked that he couldn't look at the sun long because it made his "eyes all out of breath."

Imagery, then, the picture-making quality of words, and the use of words for their sound-inducing mood are some of the aspects of poetry that the beginner-reader may explore. A wider vista will open up later, but these suffice for a beginning as well as provide discoveries that may be shared with children.

3

A Favorable Climate

To WHAT EXTENT a child's learning is influenced not only by his teacher's competence but also by the latter's attitude toward him is only a matter of speculation. Teachers have often had the experience of the arrival of a new class whose suspicion and antagonism suggest that an unfavorable relation had existed between them and their former teacher—one not conducive to learning. I once visited an extremely successful teacher whose work along creative lines drew such acclaim that her classroom became a mecca for visitors. I noted that the walls of her room were lined with paintings of hideous caricatures of people, indicating such violence of feeling that I wondered what had given rise to such an outburst. She explained that they had been painted in response to her request that the children paint the "horridest person they had ever known." "These children," she said, "came to me from a lower grade teacher who had employed excessively repressive measures to control her class, in consequence of which the children had built up a seething inner storm of resentment. I thought perhaps that if they could rid themselves of some of this feeling by channeling it off in external action, they would find relief and also present a more amenable attitude to me and to learning. You'll note," she went on, "that none of the pictures represent their old teacher." They did not—instead there was one of a threatening Hitler-like person, another of a grimacing devil, and other horrendous figures, either male or female. Apparently the children were still too frightened to risk any overt statement, but all the pictures without exception gave evidence of extreme emotions of fear and hatred.

How much relief the children derived from this channeling off I had no way of knowing, for by the time of my visit to the class, the relation between the children and their new teacher was serene, relaxed, and respectful. And I have never seen a happier or more creative group.

though the principal of the school responded with a tinge of indigna-
tion on my asking to visit this particular teacher's room, "Why does
everyone ask to see Mrs. X's creative work? The work her children do
in their regular studies is just as exceptional and outstanding."

Of course this teacher was one of those rare creative souls, the artist-
teacher, but aside from her particular gifts she had established a
"climate" in her room that any teacher may aspire to. After my visit, in
trying to analyze what such an elusive matter as climate consists of, I
came to a few conclusions. I noted the presence of a tone of mutual
respect between her and her children. In giving instructions she was
quiet and relaxed, though obviously in command of the group. Without
availing herself of the "permissiveness" too often associated with a
creative program, she accorded each child the courtesy and respect
usually reserved for adults but not so often for children. And she
listened to what they said.

This last may strike the reader as an absurd statement. Doesn't everyone listen when spoken to? Well, there are kinds of listening. One
kind is the equivalent of lip service, a superficial attention given in
passing. The other is an aroused awareness that what the child is saying
is meaningful, that it can often be for the teacher a clue that may guide
him in meeting the child's needs. It may make all the difference between the teacher's failing him and being able to extend the helping
hand that will make his next step in growth and development not only
possible but also happily inevitable.

But what such listening does for the teacher is only half the story.
His courteous respect builds in the child a sense of intrinsic worth
and the desire to be worthy of a respect generously offered. Nothing
can build security in a child more effectively than the feeling that his
teacher has an abiding regard for him. This security is of the utmost
importance in order to assure that a child may be free to apply himself
to the effort involved in learning.

For some two years I coached individual children who were having
difficulties in their school work. I was surprised to find that all the
children, no matter what their specific problems in any subject, had
one attribute in common—they were all discouraged. What this discouragement stemmed from I was not in a position to determine, though in
some instances the parents' attitude toward the child suggested the cause.
I found that what these children needed as much as, perhaps more than,

help in subject matter was a buildup of confidence in themselves and in their own ability. Surprisingly, this buildup did not require too much time to establish. Given a graduated program involving a series of small successes, the children were able to achieve the confidence that is often manifested in their slightly scornful comment, "Oh! That's easy!" Arrival at this point is the beginning of clear sailing and ultimate accomplishment.

Everything that tends to build up a child's feeling of being adequate is necessary to successful learning. For creative achievement it is essential. How can a child have access to his creative sources when he does not believe in himself? How can he dare exhibit in the open his thoughts and feelings if he denies their validity? A child's paintings and modelings may afford him a measure of anonymity, but in his poetry everything is out in the open. He has revealed himself and must take the consequences. Unless he feels assured of sympathetic understanding, he dare not give free rein to his creative impulses. But by "sympathetic understanding" I am not advocating the teacher's emotional involvement with his pupils; in fact, I would emphasize that such involvement is detrimental to children. An "impersonal-personal" relationship, so to speak, relieves the child of a sense of obligation to gratify his teacher. He is then free to address himself wholly to the task in hand without being disturbed by any inner division of feelings, while at the same time he is secure in the assurance of his teacher's support and faith.

Faith in the child is the cornerstone upon which is built a relationship that will accord him the maximum in encouragement. This faith need not be manifested in any overt expression, but where it is present it will be recognized by the child—faith in him as a person, regardless of what he may be able to accomplish. For not all children have equal intellectual ability, and a fine achievement may be the result of small effort on the part of a child gifted with words, while a mediocre achievement by a child not so gifted may represent true striving. In some subjects where the standard of *correct* and *incorrect* must be applied, as in arithmetic or spelling, a child may be rated competitively. In creative activity, such as poetry or art, high intellectual ability is not always a requisite for achievement. I have had in my classes at times children of somewhat meager ability who have been able to produce delightful poems. I had one child whose output was enormous in quantity but of poor quality. But the point I want to make is that this last child was functioning to the best of her ability, and in unrestricted fashion, in contrast to her strivings in other fields in which she could not have helped but feel her inadequacy. Do we not owe every child the opportunity to function in some area in which he does not anticipate defeat before he starts? We are overprone to value end results, whereas it is the process of functioning and the growth consequent upon functioning that are important to a child. I am not, however, unaware that teachers are required to meet certain standards in their work, but happily in the field of poetry such standards are neither required nor should they be imposed.

To return to the climate in the classroom, from which I have digressed, another factor was brought home to me. I remembered that I had nowhere seen any evidence of competition. At no time had the teacher compared one child's work to another's or singled out any child for special commendation or criticism. Acceptance, unconditional, was offered each child, and such acceptance is available to every teacher. Whatever a child presents is worthy of respectful consideration—even inept offerings, since these may be all a given child is capable of tendering. But aside from the fact that acceptance is a prime stimulus to further effort on the child's part, it provides an additional value—an immensely salutary effect on interchild relationships. As many teachers know, their class will pattern its behavior on their own: where the teacher adopts a critical attitude, the children will do likewise for two reasons—one, because criticism is the sanctioned behavior, and two, because they believe it will curry favor with him. What may be the damning effect of criticism will be dealt with later when we speak of the children's writing.

In an atmosphere of acceptance, then, the child is able to relax and does not need to bolster up whatever inadequacy he feels in himself by detraction of others. Instead, noting the teacher's appreciative response to ideas and suggestions from the children and his favorable commenting on a happy use of words in some child's poem, or a thoughtful observation, the child is inclined to accord the other children the same respect that the teacher does. A teacher will be most gratified to observe the generous acclaim with which children receive a poem which they like. One child, in an editorial meeting when the children were engaged in selecting poems to be submitted to a yearbook, said: "We shouldn't just read a poem and vote on it. Someone ought to tell the nice parts. If you don't think about it, you discard it at once, and you miss the good things." Another girl added, "It's funny—if you like it for this and don't like it for that, it spoils it to analyze." To which the first girl replied, "I think it's a good point to bring out the good parts but not the bad." As the poetry work progresses, so does the children's ability to recognize and value poetic felicities—sometimes only a word or a phrase that gives distinction to a poem.

These, then, seem to be the pillars of a room in which a climate favorable to creative work may flourish: respect, the building up of a child's faith in himself—which can only grow out of his teacher's faith in him—and acceptance which gives him the courage to be himself. The relaxation inherent in such a climate affords the child the alternative to assuming a "face" that he ordinarily feels he must present to a more or less hostile world. In the climate of such a room, a child can dare to be himself and dare to probe that self, secure in the belief that he is not only an accepted member of his world but also one who is valued for what he is regardless of what he may be able to accomplish.

4

What Poems?

CONFRONTED with the enormous body of poetry readily available, teachers are understandably at a loss concerning which poems to select for their classes. Anthologies are the most fruitful source. They are organized in a variety of ways: some merely give the names of authors and their poems in chronological order; others are organized around subject matter, as in the excellent anthology for young people, *This Singing World* by Louis Untermeyer.[1] The categories in this volume read, to name a few: Songs of Awakening, Breath of the Earth, Common Things, Places, Children, Birds and Beasts. However, neither of the two types of organization will be particularly helpful to the teacher. In his search for poems appropriate to his age group he will of necessity have to select those best suited to his own children.

While there is a difference between the poems suitable for seven- and eight-year-olds and for children of ten and older, certain common principles may guide the teacher in his choice. The first, mentioned in an earlier chapter, is that poems should deal with experience familiar to children. In the main, the poems should have been written in comparatively recent times, since these treat of a world with which our children are acquainted. An exception to this restriction is poetry of the nature of Robert Louis Stevenson's, whose *A Child's Garden of Verses* taps the more or less ageless preoccupations of childhood. Poems of today likewise employ a vocabulary more readily understandable than that of earlier times. The teacher will find that children respond to poems about natural phenomena—the sun, the moon, rain, rivers, animals—as well as to poems of personal experience such as "Afternoon on a Hill," previously quoted. It is advisable that poems should be chosen that may be grasped at a first hearing. Any poem containing too many unfamiliar words tends to disrupt interest, though at times a poem

[1] (New York: Harcourt, Brace & World, 1926.)

22

may contain one or two words that are foreign to a child's vocabulary. This fact need not be a deterrent to the choice of that particular poem, since the enlarging of a child's vocabulary is a worthy by-product of the poetry study. Difficult words may be explained before reading the poem.

The length of a poem is another matter that should be taken into consideration. For the younger children poems should be short, since any too protracted demand on attention is fatal to interest.

I would suggest that poetry of the jingle variety be only infrequently presented—not that all jingle is to be decried. The delightful verses of A. A. Milne, like the nursery rhymes, are appropriate in their place, but in the classroom they are too facile and serve to identify poetry in the child's mind with verse that adheres to a certain bouncy rhythm. Many children have arrived in my classes convinced that nothing is poetry that is not of the "Dee-dum, dee-dum, dee-dum, dee-dee / Dee-dum, dee-dum, dee-dum, you see" variety, so that it takes some time to displace this concept with a more valid one. What actually constitutes poetry need not be overtly defined. Through the years no definition of poetry that is all inclusive and universally acceptable has been, or perhaps ever will be, arrived at.

But infallibly the children learn to sense the nature of poetry when they have been exposed to it over a period of time. An identical phrase has cropped up surprisingly often in different classes. Commenting on a poem of their own or on that of another child, they say, "That sounds more like a story than a poem." What they are sensing by this observation is that something more than blunt statement is necessary in a poem—that there exists such a thing as "prosiness," though they are unable to formulate the concept. They sense also that the absence of cadence is detrimental to poetic expression. Cadence is an elusive thing to define, but here again there is no need to attempt a definition with the children. They eventually recognize consciously that absence of cadence may make the difference between what is and what is not a poem, as more specific commentary than the one noted above appears during the progress of the poetry study.

A ten-year-old girl writes:

> The moon is like a silver plate.
> It breaks as some one breaks a real one.

> Other times it is put together again
> By strong fingers of sky and clouds.

On rereading this at the session following its writing, she says, "It is not good," and amends it to read:

> The moon is like a silver plate.
> It is broken by strong fingers of sky and clouds,
> And then put together by them again.[2]

While not notably poetic, the latter version is an obvious improvement over the first. The child has recognized the prosy ineptitude of line two. We shall have more to say of the children's development of criteria later. At this point what we want to bring home is the fact that children have, perhaps instinctively, a keen sense of what constitutes poetry not only in rhythmic but in free verse as well.

In order to further such recognition it is advisable to read to the children a considerable amount of free verse. So much of modern poetry falls into this category that there is a wide field upon which to draw. In the absence of regular rhythm and rhyme the children learn to focus attention on the essentials of poetry; and this concentration is of especial value to them when they come to write their own poems.[3] Regular rhyme and rhythm are difficult to handle. The attempt to manipulate their thoughts and feelings into a rigid framework forces the children to distort their spontaneous expression and resort to other undesirable practices, all of which will be discussed when we speak of the writing program.

By advocating the choice of much free verse I do not wish to imply the exclusion of rhythmic verse. The response to rhythm is basic in all people, and a great deal of aesthetic enjoyment of poetry rests upon an either unconscious or conscious realization of its presence. I advocate the choice of much free verse not only that the children may feel the sanction to write in this form but also because heretofore emphasis in

---

[2] These two versions are from Flora J. Arnstein, *Children Write Poetry* (New York: Dover Publications, Inc., 1967).

[3] Sean, a twelve-year-old, says: "A poem with regular rhythm and rhyme sometimes distracts you from the idea by the rhythm. With free verse you notice the meaning." And Rachel adds, "Sometimes words are put in just to rhyme, and that ruins it."

the teaching of poetry has been placed almost exclusively upon rhythm and rhyme, so that other aspects of poetry often have been overlooked.

Another caution with regard to choice is perhaps not necessary, but attention might be drawn to the fact that a great deal of poetry for children tends at times to a certain archness and is "written down" to them. In accordance with what I have previously said of maintaining a respectful attitude towards children, I feel that poetry of this order violates such respect. The first acts on the assumption that "cuteness" is acceptable to children and that it is a desirable quality to foster; the second, that children are not capable of a serious approach to poetry. Of course not all poetry written for children presents these undesirable aspects, and the teacher of young children especially will need to draw upon some of these, since the amount of poetry understandable to young children is necessarily limited.

For the older children narrative verse and ballads prove most acceptable and, as the poetry program continues, poems demanding thought and presenting increasing use of poetic devices may be offered. The teacher will indeed be surprised to find that children are able to come to grips with poems he would have initially believed to be far beyond their understanding.

5

How Young?

THE SIX-YEAR-OLDS enter my classroom wide-eyed and somewhat dubious. Shepherded by their class teacher, who aware of the poetry work taking place throughout the school has asked me to read poetry with her group, they take their places around our ample table. I myself have certain misgivings. I have never taught such young children, but I reassure myself with the thought that they cannot be too different from my seven-year-olds. In any case, that which has guided my choice of poems for the sevens will apply no doubt as well to the younger children.

However, another factor enters here. Because I shall not have continuous contact with these children, I cannot plan any long-range program for them. Since our meetings will be few and occasional, my aim must be restricted to making poetry immediately pleasurable, so that the idea of poetry may have only happy connotations for them. Of course pleasure should be one of the concomitants of the poetry experience for all ages; with these particular children it may have to be the end-all.

I decide to read one poem which has proved "sure-fire" for the sevens and even for some of the older children, "Jonathan Bing" by B. Curtis Brown.[1] Though it is a type of poem I have cautioned against in my last chapter, it is one that fills the need on certain occasions. Before reading it I ask the children whether they forget things sometimes. Up go the hands as each child is impatient to tell some instance of his forgetfulness. When all have had the opportunity to speak, I say, "Here is what one poet had to say about forgetting."

[1] From *One Hundred Best Poems for Boys and Girls*, compiled by Marjorie Barrows, Whitman Publishing Company, Racine, Wisconsin. This book is out of print, but perhaps it can be found in some libraries.

JONATHAN BING

Poor old Jonathan Bing
Went out in his carriage to visit the King,
But everyone pointed and said, "Look at that!
Jonathan Bing has forgotten his hat!"
    (He'd forgotten his hat!)

Poor old Jonathan Bing
Went home and put on a new hat for the King,
But up by the palace a soldier said, "Hi!
You can't see the King; you've forgotten your tie!"
    (He'd forgotten his tie!)

Poor old Jonathan Bing
He put on a beautiful tie for the King,
But when he arrived an Archbishop said, "Ho!
You can't come to court in pyjamas, you know!"

Poor old Jonathan Bing
Went home and addressed a short note to the King:
"If you please will excuse me I won't come to tea,
For home's the best place for all people like me!"

The procedure of introducing a poem by discussion of the experience with which it deals is one I consistently employ. It sets the stage for the poem and relates the child to the experience and hence to the poem's content.

Here let me interpolate that, as I go along, I shall necessarily refer to certain of my own procedures which seemed to foster favorable results. However, I want to disclaim any pretense of presenting these as "a method." Reducing procedures to a hard-and-fast mold robs them of life; it is far better for a teacher to experiment, to employ his own approach than to accept literally the formula of another. What works with one person may not work with the next. Unlike the teaching of arithmetic, for which a method may be outlined, the teaching of art is most successful when the teacher ventures into paths of his own choosing. If he is sensitive to the children's responses and flexible enough to discard procedures that prove headed in the wrong direction, he is more likely to be successful—for the more creative the teacher, the more creative the child will be. I suggest, then, that the practices I shall describe may be most happily regarded as a jumping-off place for the teacher's individual venture.

There are innumerable approaches to teaching, and some that are congenial to one teacher may not be so to another. The artist-teacher to whom I referred in an earlier chapter made use of a diametrically different approach from my own. Whereas she was a very dynamic person who was able to carry the children along on the wave of her own enthusiasm, I am inclined to be retiring and resort to drawing the children out. But the difference in our ways of working diminishes in no respect my regard for her achievement. Certain practices of Hughes Mearns, as described in his *Creative Youth*, I admire unreservedly, but they would be impossible for me to apply.

In the *English Journal* for April, 1951, Marjorie Braymer wrote of her experience in the teaching of poetry to reluctant high school students. Her approach was novel. She started by exploring the role that poetry has played in the lives of primitive and civilized peoples: "how poetry evolved to meet man's need for songs that would make bearable the monotony of hard labor." She dealt with the "historical and psychological reasons for poetry in everyday life." And when she had established for her students the validity of poetry, she embarked upon the discussion of the nature of poetry, of different forms of poetry, of layers of meaning, until she had not only won over her class to poetry but had also developed a group of enthusiastic explorers who were bringing to class new discoveries of their own. The titles of some of their papers speak for themselves: "The Truth of Poetry"; "A Precious Discovery"; "Poetry Is Fun"; " 'Growing Up' about Poetry"; "A Change of Attitude." So, I repeat, what in this book I have to offer is merely my personal approach along with whatever my experience has taught me.

To return to "Jonathan Bing." Some of the qualities in this poem may suggest to the teacher poems of a similar nature suitable for young children. At this age children delight in rhythm—it is, perhaps, as much the rhythmic quality of *Mother Goose* as its content that has endeared it to children over the years. "Jonathan Bing" has just such a seductive rhythm and attractive rhymes as well. At times, on a second reading, I have read the first line of the rhymed couplets and then omitted the rhyming word of the second, which the children have shown great gusto in supplying. The poem contains repetition, so dear to young children's hearts, and a humor which appeals especially to them. Finally, it deals with the experience of forgetting, shared alike by young and old.

Having won over the children to poetry, the teacher may turn from the type of poem quoted to poems of a more serious content. "Who Has Seen the Wind?" by Christina Rossetti provides discussion for the experience of a windy day. "Tired Tim" and "The Little Green Orchard" by Walter de la Mare draw upon child experience, and "Fog" by Carl Sandburg might be an introduction to free verse.

After reading a poem I have found it a valuable practice to ask the children what they have noticed in the poem. I do not favor paraphrasing, the saying of a poem "in your own words." The words of a poem and what the poem says are really one—to say a poem in different words is to destroy it as a poem. But to ask the children what they have noticed serves to whet their attention. They are eager to enumerate all the "things" they have noticed, and I have found that after a little practice eight-year-olds are able to recall the entire content of a poem. In order to refresh memory they frequently ask for a second reading, which is of course to be desired. What one can "do" with a poem in the teaching of young children is necessarily limited, but a pleasurable introduction to poetry is in any case a worthy aim.

My work with this particular group of six-year-olds was of short duration because of the conflict in their teacher's schedule and mine. But some years later I had the pleasure of reading poetry with another group of the same age. We began the program with the making of books. How this procedure suggested itself to me I do not remember, but it proved so far-reaching in results that I adopted it with all subsequent classes. Stiff-covered blank books, a selection of attractive cotton materials with which to cover them, spatulas, vegetable glue, and colored paper for lining the inside covers were the only equipment necessary. After the children had made their choice from among the materials, they settled down to the business of covering the books.

The making of these books has a particular value for the teacher. Observing the children working provides him with the opportunity of getting acquainted with a new group, noting their characteristics, the differences between those who go about the work confidently and those who are tentative and require help and encouragement. Also the book-making provides an informal atmosphere, one in which the children can be themselves without self-consciousness. For the children it affords an activity that all ages enjoy and has the added advantage of engaging each child immediately and sending off the poetry hour to a pleasurable start. Two sessions are generally necessary for the younger children to finish their books, the first for pasting the outer covers, the second to add the linings. Of course after both sessions the books must be pressed under heavy volumes or any other weights available.

Many teachers have classes of such a size that the making of books is not feasible. I used these procedures in poetry classes of about sixteen children. However, another procedure is open to the teacher of large classes—he may procure an attractive book in which children may paste poems he brings to class. The object of the books in both cases is to provide a more personal anthology than is represented by published anthologies. These last cannot offer the child the personal, intimate feeling that arises from a collection of poems of his own choice; often anthologies contain many poems unsuitable to a child's age, hence neither invite nor foster reading.

I have referred above to poems brought to class. What are these poems that are destined for the books? At each session I would read a number of poems from which the children would make a choice. I would type these and bring them to the succeeding session for the children to paste in their books. The opportunity for the exercise of choice I believe to be of prime importance. Choice is the first step in the development of "appreciation." I place *appreciation* in quotes, as I am somewhat wary of so-called appreciation classes in the arts. Appreciation, I believe, cannot be taught. Along with the development of taste, it results from growth, from maturing, and from the exposure to poetry and the opportunity to write. Any designation of a work of art as "good" or "bad" is only confusing to a child. Criteria supplied from without have no meaning because to a child they seem arbitrary, and an acceptance of them without understanding leads more often than not to misapplication. But more of this will be said when we deal later with the children's writing.

What a child likes, then, is a valid base upon which to build appreciation. Because of the expectation of having to make a choice from among the poems read, the children's initial attention is aroused and focused, and often this same expectation leads to the request for the rereading of certain poems, as has been already mentioned. The advantage of such rereading need not be labored. Altogether the exercise of choosing implies an act of discrimination, and discrimination has its value even if this is only the expression of personal preference.

The teacher of a large class is obviously not able to type poems for individual books, but for the class book it may not be too burdensome for him to write or type single poems. After a reading at a particular session he might ask the group to vote on the poem they liked best, and the majority's choice would then be included in the class book. A careful distinction should, however, be made. The children should not be asked to vote for the "best" poem—since the evaluation of a poem as good or bad is not within their ability—but they should be invited to say which one they *liked* best. And I suggest that the children be not required to copy the chosen poem, since, as I mentioned earlier, anything that savors of a chore should be avoided in the poetry program. Of course if a child volunteers to copy a poem, that is another matter. Each child may be allowed his turn to paste the poem in the class book, which would make him a participant, to a certain extent, in the compiling of the anthology.

After the entering of the poem in the book, the teacher might read the poem aloud with this particular child. There is a good reason for not permitting children to read the poems alone. A stumbling rendition is fatal to a poem, but even when a child reads fluently, he is not equipped to give due value to certain words or to pauses, or to other aspects of the poem: needless to say a poem should always be presented in its best light. By reading with the teacher, the child learns the appropriate pace, for poetry usually should be read more slowly than prose. I explain to the children that, whereas in a story the author is eager to carry the reader along with the story's progress, in a poem what the poet desires is to have the reader linger, so that he may enjoy the words, the pictures, and get the feeling of the poem. Thus the children acquire the habit of reading a poem slowly and quietly. One little girl in her eagerness to conform to these requirements read a poem in such a subdued, almost unintelligible manner as to bring forth the comment from another child: "It's all right to read quietly, but she doesn't need to read as if she is a ghost!"

Many readers of poetry adopt a somewhat self-conscious or declamatory rendition. Either they pause overlong at line endings, or too scrupulously do not pause at all in such run-on lines as Tennyson's:

Till the great sea snake under the sea
From his coiled sleeps in the central deeps
Would slowly trail himself sevenfold
Round the hall where I sate . . .

Now the fact that a line ends at a certain place, in free verse as well as in metrical, suggests that there is a reason for its so doing. The new line may imply a certain emphasis, since a word in this position acquires a slight stress, or it may mean that a breath is taken, or the line ending may accentuate the rhyme (sleeps and deeps) in the quotation above, or a number of other reasons may be responsible for certain lines ending at specific places. I feel that a fraction of a pause should occur at line endings—perhaps the equivalent to the ears of what the moving to the following line entails to the eyes. What I am trying to say is that a poem should not be pedantically read in accordance with preconceived ideas. A simple forthright reading invites the readiest interest and response, since children react negatively to anything that savors of affectation.

My own poetry sessions after a time fell into something of the regularity of a routine: a familiar framework which, when flexible enough to allow some variation, provided the children with the security of the known and expected. Each session started with pasting in the books the poems chosen at the previous session and their reading them aloud—in unison with those who had chosen the same poem and with me. Then followed the reading of new poems, generally not more than four, as this number allowed time for discussion, reading, and choosing. In all, the procedure involved approximately twenty minutes, at which point I brought the lesson to a close—unless the children had embarked upon writing. How the writing came about will now be taken up in our consideration of the seven- and eight-year-olds.

6

We Like to Write

FOR THE PAST YEAR a group of four twelve-year-olds, two boys and two girls, have been coming to my home once a week to read poetry. We started as a summer project last year, but the children asked to continue during the winter and now have expressed the desire to go on into next year. This would seem to argue that they like poetry. Said one of the boys, "When my mother wanted me to start, I thought I would hate it. I thought poetry was 'sissy' stuff. Now I like it—and writing is the best part." This remark is the first overt expression of liking to write that has come from any child I have taught, but the fact that I have accumulated some sixteen typed volumes of poems the children have written over the years corroborates what this boy has said.

Getting young children to write is not so difficult as some teachers might imagine. Given the room climate earlier referred to and a period of time devoted to the reading of poetry, during which no mention of writing has been made, the children take the next step naturally in their stride. The request to write has often followed upon my bringing to class a book of Hilda Conkling's poems. The picture of the little girl on the frontispiece and the fact that her poems had been accorded the dignity of a printed book impressed the children greatly and brought forth the spontaneous question, "Can't we write some poems?" Previously it had been explained to them that Hilda's "writing" did not mean that she actually had transcribed the poems herself but that she had dictated them to her mother. The children then naturally assumed that they would dictate their poems to me.

It became amply evident by the unself-consciousness with which the children unburdened themselves in their poems that they enjoyed expressing and sharing their thoughts and feelings. They would write of anything that came to mind, and quite simply, for they were not as yet

33

hampered, as were some of the older children, by any preconceived ideas of what is and what is not poetry. Reading these poems, teachers, however, may be inclined to question "Is any of this poetry? And if not, of what use is it?" They may be reassured. If this is not poetry, it is the stuff of which poetry is made, and the writing of it affords the child the opportunity and the sanction for tapping his own creative sources. I have had two children in my poetry class for as long as five years, others for not such extended periods, but all long enough to indicate that these early poems are the preliminary exercises, the gropings toward a more authentic poetic expression. And many of these young children's poems might be considered poetry in their own right.

The business of dictating involves a practical problem: how to occupy the other children when one child is dictating. My solution was to ask each child to raise his hand when ready to dictate and to call each to my desk in turn. While waiting, the other children are preoccupied with the poem they have in mind, thinking it through and trying to remember it. But after dictation, then what? I have generally made available several books of poems for the children to look through, or I have permitted them to continue with any book they may have been currently reading.

The teacher of large classes has an additional problem. He may have to do some organizing in advance, perhaps by dividing his group into two, allowing one group to read or pursue some other school activity while addressing himself to the other group. It is of course necessary that quiet be preserved, an atmosphere of relaxation, for the "poetry-feeling" to be achieved. Or a teacher might explain to all the children that each will have the opportunity to dictate, even if all will not be able to do so at one session. Or one period may be given to poetry reading, another to writing. A resourceful teacher may feel his way for the best procedures.

Of prime importance is the manner in which the teacher receives the child's poems, because upon his attitude will hinge the continuance of the child's writing. If the teacher is unresponsive to what the child produces in his first halting attempts, the child is forced to reject his ideas and feelings and to substitute for his spontaneity something he feels will be acceptable to his teacher, if indeed he will make any further attempt to write. Too great expectancy of him beyond his immediate ability discourages further effort, and, since our aim is to enable him to continue to develop his powers, as teachers we should accept whatever a child writes at a given time as valid for him at that stage in his development. I have heard many teachers say to a child, "You could do better," but who knows what any child can do? I have been surprised too often by superior performance to guess a child's potential.

In what manner, then, should a teacher receive a child's poem? It would seem that all that is necessary is a favorable response, worded somewhat vaguely, such as "That is nice" or "I like that." The children, I have found, neither expect nor desire more. Actually many walk away from the desk while still dictating, and many do not recognize the poems of their own writing when these are read at a later session. Praise or comment is not required. Unless children have become accustomed to expect praise for everything they do, they treat their poems as casually as they do a finished arithmetic assignment. And this is as it should be. However, at times it is advisable for the teacher to draw attention to Johnny's accurate observation as illustrated in his poem or to Jane's well-chosen words in a description. Such observations may be made provided they are done lightly and that the child is not made to feel singled out for praise. The justification for comment in these cases is that indirectly the children are led to sense that a certain accuracy of observation and a happy use of words are desirable elements in writing. At the same time the light, impersonal character of the observation does not lead to any competitive feelings. It might not be amiss to state here that such indirect teaching tends to bring about results unobtainable by head-on instruction. There is little that can be dogmatically taught children in the creative pursuit of poetry. There are no "rights" and "wrongs" in the sense that a word is spelled correctly or incorrectly. Rather there are desirable modes of expression, but these cannot be formulated step by step or reduced to formal "rules." Instead, what is desirable can only be suggested indirectly by attention being drawn to certain acceptable practices. The child then makes his own inferences and incorporates in his writing as much of the suggestion that at the time he is able to assimilate. An example of indirect approach may be found in our earlier discussion of the word "tottering" in the poem, "The Pasture." It would be ill-advised to enjoin the child to search for words of comparable effectiveness in his own writing. Such a conscious search would block the spontaneity one wishes to preserve and foster, since it is just this spontaneous expression that provides the groundwork upon which the child can build.

An adult poet, mature in the practice of his craft, often substitutes a dynamic word for one that is dead or shopworn, but even for him the *trouvé* word comes by the grace of God. All of us make use of the phrase, "It just came to me," without questioning the authenticity of ideas arrived at without deliberate planning. The best we teachers can offer the child is the opportunity to draw upon his native gifts in an atmosphere in which they may continue to flourish. We need not be concerned if some of what "comes" in the beginning is awkward or naïve. For it is only by the exercise of his own powers that a child becomes proficient; Hughes Mearns speaks of the "muddy water" that must be allowed to flow before the stream becomes clear.

The poems of some six-year-olds are appended here to give the teacher an idea of what may be expected of children of this age. He may expect to find certain modes of expression appearing again and again, not only at this age but later in the poems of the sevens and eights. One of these is exemplified in the tendency of a child to fall into stereotypes. For example, John begins every poem with the phrase, "It's fun to . . ."

> It's fun to sail.
> As I watch all the sights,
> Miles and miles away.
> It's fun to walk on the deck
> And watch the sailors scrub and rub the boat.
> It's fun to sail,
> Especially when you're going to strange docks.

Karen begins her series of poems with, "When I . . ."

> When I am sick in bed,
> I always put out all the toys I have,
> And play and play till I have to put them away,
> And I don't want to.

After a short time she relinquishes the "When I's" for another repeated expression: "I have . . ."

> I have a little book.
> I wonder what's in it.

I'll read it out loud
So I'll know what's in it . . .
Then I'll know what's in it.

Mary Anne starts all of her poems "Once when . . ."

Once when I went to the beach,
I played in the sand,
And then went in the water,
And when the waves came up and splashed,
They felt so good.
And when it was time to go home,
I didn't want to.

The teacher need not be concerned about this repetition and feel he
ought to direct the children into other modes of expression. Repetition
at this point may answer some need of the children who employ it. In
any case, without comment from the teacher, the children of their own
accord relinquish stereotypes when these apparently have served their
purpose.

Beginning writers are inclined to dictate little stories that bear small
relation to poetry. Jane dictates:

A ROSE AND A BUTTERFLY

The butterfly was sitting on the rose,
And the little girl came and scared it away.
The butterfly flew away to a palm tree,
And then a boy climbed up the palm tree,
And scared the butterfly away.
Then it found another plant.
It flew into the bramble bushes,
And a boy climbed again in the bramble bushes.
He scared the butterfly away.
The butterfly this time got the boy away from him—
He went up on top of an incinerator.

The incinerator delightfully proclaims its independence of anything
poetic. That stories occur in the poems of the seven-year-olds is not
surprising, for until the children have been exposed to poetry they
naturally write in the prose forms to which they have been accustomed.

It is also possible that most of the poems they have heard have been narrative ones.

Many children, however, draw upon the subject matter of lyric poetry: they write of nature, of the objects around them, and of their own reactions to these. Martha writes:

> Magic chair, can you walk?
> Can anybody sit in you?
> Could I sit in you?
> Do you have any friends around the living room?
> Could you walk down the streets
> With your little bare feets?
> Do you talk to the lamp,
> The big old lamp in front of you?
> When do you eat, old magic chair,
> What do you eat today?

Martha has a vivid imagination. She invests inanimate objects with human qualities as in the following poem:

> Old house, are you lonely,
> With no windows in your window-pane,
> In the tree-tops down in the forest alone?
> Does anybody come to stay in you?
> The breezes ask you.

This has a genuine lyric quality rare in such a young child; one has only to compare the cadence with that of the previous poem.

Rachel also has a lyric feeling:

> When it's morning I wake up,
> And say I had a long, long dream.
> And I go in the sun
> And it's blooming like sky,
> And it's sunny and the flowers are starting to grow.
> Then my poor nice day started to rain,
> 'Cause I was going to a little tea-party.
> After the tea-party the sun came out,
> And the flowers started to bloom again,
> Then they started to go down,
> 'Cause night was coming.

Rachel seems a bit hazy about the relation of sun, rain, and night to flowers, but the sun "blooming like sky" is a charming lyric touch.

Many children inject subjective matter into their poems as does Kenny in the following:

> The black clouds are flying in the dark sky.
> At first they are white, when they are in the sky,
> When the wind is blowing them.
> Then I go to sleep at night.
> Suddenly the windows start banging and banging,
> And the dark clouds
> Throw great little pieces of ice down,
> And they hit the street,
> And make the street all white.
> Then it starts to pour,
> And the rain taps on the window
> Forever and forever until the rain is stopped.

He continues this with a prosy schedule of getting up, breakfast, and play, but in the portion of the poem quoted here is indication of observation of color and sound along with the childlike phrase, "great little pieces of ice."

In the following poem, which incidentally is the longest a child of any age has written in my classes, he again gives evidence of acute observation and a dramatic quality of a somewhat breathless variety.

> The firemen slide down the pole.
> They jump onto the engine.
> The siren blows.
> The firemen hang on tight.
>
> One sits in the driver's seat and drives the engine
> As fast as it can go.
> Sometimes they turn around the corner so fast,
> They turn on two wheels.
>
> When they get to the fire
> They ask the chief what they're 'sposed to do.
> The chief is already there.
> He has a bright red coat and so do they,
> And a bright shiny bell,
> And bright red lights,
> And so do they have bright red lights.

Clang, clang goes the hook-and-ladder truck,
Going down the street as fast as it can go.
There's a man in back of the engine
With a steering wheel,
And he's strapped on top of the ladders.

When they get to the fire they set up a ladder,
Right up to the building.
The flames shoot out every place in the building.
The firemen take a hose and put it right up the building.

They take an axe and run up the ladder,
And chop the burning pieces of the wood.
Sometimes they have to get up late at night,
And the roaring engine comes out,
And the siren blows as loud as it can.
Sometimes they have to do it on foggy nights.
Sometimes when they're doing it on foggy nights,
Boats catch on fire,
And they hear the fog horns tooting to make them hurry.
Sometimes they have to have a lot of fireboats come,
'Cause lots of boats have a wreck,
And they all catch on fire,
So a tug boat has to come and pull them,
So a fireman can get in between the boats,
And get water from the bay and the ocean.
Sometimes they're in the bay or the ocean,
    The Pacific Ocean.

Sometimes they have to get a search light
On the foggy nights to see where they are,
So they won't let the fire burn worse.
Sometimes the bridge gets on fire,
And they have to come very fast.
Sometimes the bridge breaks on them,
And then they have to get water from the ocean,
And when the bridge breaks the fire is out.[1]

Only the fact that at this point the class period came to an end put a stop to Kenny's "inspiration." But he was not discouraged. We met

[1] From Flora J. Arnstein, *Children Write Poetry* (New York: Dover Publications, Inc., 1967).

almost a month later and he continued (without having heard a repeat of his poem) with another thirty lines on the same subject. By this time he has come around to forest fires and his poem ends:

> Sometimes about three months, the place where the fire was
> Is still scorching, sometimes more.
> And sometimes when it's still scorching,
> Cigars and cigarettes are thrown from a road,
> And that starts another big fire,
> And burns up the things that are scorching.

Aside from being unusually articulate for a child of six, Kenny demonstrates a characteristic common to the poems of young children—that of exploring a subject from many angles; though it must be said no child has been so thorough in exploration as he.

Susan is another able child. She dictates:

> The rose is pink in the spring,
> It turns yellow in the summer,
> And the butterfly that stands on it
> Looks velvet.
>
> The roses that are pretty in the garden
> Sometimes yellow, red and pink,
> And the violets look so pretty—
> The purple ones like velvet,
> And the white ones like silk.
>
> And sometimes the pansies' green stems and yellow.
> The country is full of all those pretty flowers,
> But still I can't decide which of the flowers I like the best.
> But I think all day long,
> But I can't think in the night,
> Because I'm sleeping.
>
> And all the flowers have green stems,
> But some have purple stems—
> I don't know which ones have purple stems.
> And the daphne smells so good,
> And so do gardenias, and so do roses,
> But gardenias and roses and daphnes look pretty—
> I wonder why the little daphne
> Sparkles so in the sunshine.

In this poem Susan forecasts many modes of expression which will appear with great frequency in the poems of the seven- and eight-year-old children. One is that of enumeration. Susan enumerates the different flowers, their different colors, and the different colors of the stems. However, she enumerates somewhat incidentally, whereas the older children often start their poems with enumerative lists. It is as though at this age children are impelled to assemble all the data that they know on a given subject in order to be able to envisage it.

The expression "I like" is another one common to the older children—which Susan touches upon here in her inability to decide on her preference between the different flowers. The "I like's" may serve in some way to relate the child to phenomena outside him; in any case the use of the phrase is too common to be dismissed as of no significance. Susan also evaluates her subjects in terms of aesthetic appeal: the flowers are pretty; the daphne smells good. Like Kenny she has a staying power unusual in children even of a later age; she is not deflected from her subject.

All in all, the poem has the charm of childhood in its minuteness and freshness of observation, but in addition Susan avails herself of one of the essential devices of poetry, imagery. The butterfly "looks like velvet"; the "purple violets like velvet, the white ones like silk." And the poem ends on the delightful query of why the daphne "sparkles" in the sun.

These, then, are some of the poems of six-year-olds. What the sevens write now follows.

7

The Sevens and Eights

THE SEVENS AND EIGHTS are eager and articulate. They write about what they see, hear, touch, or feel inwardly. Inanimate objects, nature, animals engage their attention; in fact there is nothing that is not grist to their mill. They assess the world about them and their own relation to it. Fay at eight writes:

MOON

When I go to bed at night,
I turn off my light
And I look at the beautiful moon
And the thousand pretty little stars,
When the sky is clear.

Eric at seven also writes about nature:

The clouds are so fluffy and white.
I wonder if they're strong enough to lie down on,
And maybe if they're strong enough,
I might sit on one and sing myself a song.
If I sat on a cloud I might see a twittering bird,
Or maybe a robin flying toward the south.
And maybe I might see a plane
With its glistening wings
As it goes sailing by.

Roger at eight:

RAIN

The rain pours down upon the leaves
While I lie in bed.
I hear the leaves rustling in the night,
And when I get up in the morning,
I see everything wet with bubbles all around.

43

Eric now turns his attention to

A TRAIN ON A JOURNEY

A train is in the railroad yard.
It is going on a great long journey
It is off on its way now.
Where does it go?
The winds are passing—
They whistle, they sing a song,
And this is what they sing:
"Go fast, go fast, you're on your way."
"Oo, Oo," this is what I sing—
"Oo, Oo."

These poems deriving from direct experience are a far cry from the poems of children printed in so-called "Kiddie Columns." Recently I heard a radio program of children reading and discussing their poems under the leadership of a woman who could not have been their teacher for, among other questions, she asked under what circumstances the poems had been written. The program, with its implied achievement and the importance given to the poems by the questions asked, seemed to me to be the most ill-advised procedure for the children, who were made to feel that they were in some way especially gifted. Their poems did not bear out this assumption. They were facile jingles that bore no relation to genuine experience—the sort any bright child can turn out a dime a dozen. In contrast, the poems I have quoted above represent children's natural preoccupations and have none of the pretentiousness that invariably arises when children are made to feel self-conscious about their writing.

Ellen at eight writes:

A BEAUTIFUL COLOR

Blue is a beautiful color.
Blue is in the waters of lakes,
Rivers, streams and oceans.
And the sky is blue.
A flame is blue.
Just as the flowers are.
Blue is in the most beautiful things
In the world.

While I make no great claims for this as poetry, I should like to contrast it with an adult poem on the same subject. Placing them side by side may serve to illuminate that elusive matter of sentimentality I referred to in an earlier chapter.

BLUE

So many radiant things are blue—
Heavens of fragile turquoise tint;
This curling smoke, a sea-ward view;
The eyes of laughing girls, that hint
Of sudden stars or sun-touched dew;
So many dear, delightful things—
Forget-me-nots, and gentians, too;
A blue-bird's crisp and curving wings—
I think the soul's own hidden hue
Must be some lovely shade of blue!

Let us note first the trite adjectives the adult poet employs: *radiant* (as applied to "things"—with the noun's lack of specificity); *fragile, curling* (of smoke), *sun-touched* (dew), *curving* (wings)—not a fresh observation is among them; nothing is seen with the individual eye. Then let us note the blue objects the author has chosen to enumerate and contrast these with those the child has noted: *heavens,* as against the child's more direct *sky; stars, dew,* the sentiment-laden *forget-me-nots* and the eyes of *laughing girls,* as against the child's fresh observation of the blue of a *flame* and the straightforward *flowers.* The banal ending caps a poem that is further removed from true poetry than is the unpretentious one of the child. For poetry is that which is seen and experienced at first hand. The child is writing out of experience; the adult, in language that suggests less a personal reaction than one derived from the parlor gift book.

The poems quoted above are less common than the usual poems written by children of the same age. As mentioned in the previous chapter, the children employ certain recurrent types of expression, such as enumeration which recurs with surprising frequency in the poems of the sevens and eights. No teacher need be told that measurement by chronological age is far from accurate, that some children at seven have a mental age of nine or more, and conversely, a child without really being less able, may perform at an age level younger than his own. In the creative field these variations are especially pronounced. What may seem to be reluctance or unreadiness in any given child may occur when he has been cut off from his creative self, either by some emotional disturbance or by any of a number of other causes. Cultural factors enter the picture as well. A child from an environment where reading is a matter of course, and one who has read widely by himself, will have at his command a vocabulary and a handling of language that are not available to children with a more limited cultural background. Hence the age designations employed in this book should be regarded more as a convenience of classification than as an indication of what children at any given age may write.

Enumeration, though, seems especially characteristic of the sevens and eights. That the children are not imitating one another, as might be surmised, is evidenced by the fact that this mode of expression arises spontaneously in different groups at different times and places. The process of assembling all the data they know on one subject seems to be a phase of development through which children pass. Here follow some typical examples.

John at seven writes:

> There are all kinds of animals:
> There are brown animals,
> Red animals, and yellow animals.
> There are some funny animals,
> And there are some baby animals.
> There are animals that have big, big noses,
> And big feet, like the pelicans.

Emily at seven writes:

> Books, books,
> Red books, yellow books,
> Orange books,
> All sorts of kinds of color books.
> Sometimes there are magazines,
> In the shelves of the library.
> Usually there are.
> There are yellow, blue, red magazines,
> And orange magazines,
> Not only books and magazines,
> But fairy tales.

Adolph at eight enumerates:

> Flowers are growing,
> And some are yellow,
> And some are red,
> And some are blue,
> And some are big,
> And some are little.
> The sun makes them grow.
> At night-time they go to sleep,
> And let their little heads hang down.

In the last three lines the child makes some general observations accompanying enumeration, and this variation occurs in many of the poems.

Kay at seven dictates:

> There are big horses
> And little horses,
> There are horses that are wild,
> And horses that buck,
> And you cannot ride them
> Unless you ride very, very well.
> There are tame horses
> That ride very smoothly.
> Mostly little children ride ponies.
> Ponies mostly don't buck.
> I would like to ride a pony, but I cannot,
> For I don't know how to ride.

Along with poems containing general statements appear other forms of expression: "I like" or "I love." Among the seven-year-olds there occur in the course of three terms 67 instances of the use of the former, and in the eight-year-olds in five terms 104. In the nine-year-olds in six terms the expression occurs 61 times, and from then on it tapers off with only occasional appearances in the poems of older children. It is as though in the employment of these expressions the children were relating themselves in terms of feeling to their subject matter and at the same time, by expressing preference, envisaging it in a subjective rather than objective fashion.

The following by a seven-year-old is a poem in point. It starts with the familiar list, then expresses a preference.

TREES

There are big trees and little trees,
There are eucalyptus trees and pine trees.
I like the eucalyptus trees better
Because they are more healthy
And smell better.

Whether this little boy likes the eucalyptus trees because they are healthy themselves or presumably because he believes them to be wholesome for people is engagingly ambiguous.

The same boy in a few months progresses from strict enumeration and the blunt statement "I like" to a more extended assembling of data, and from the expression of personal preference to a commentary on the behavior of other people.

FLOWERS

There are all kinds of flowers
In the big garden—
Marigolds, pansies, roses
And other flowers.
They grow in the spring,
And go down in the autumn.
I should think they'd stay up
All the year,
But they do not.
When you forget to water them,
And you forget to pull out the weeds,
They die—they die of thirst
And of the weeds.
I think it is very cruel,
But some other people do not.

Long, long ago
I had a very big garden
With all these flowers,
And they all died,
And we never, never wanted to see them again.[1]

---

[1] Hughes Mearns in his *The Creative Adult* comments upon this poem, as well as on my teaching.

Ellen, aged eight, also makes the transition from mere listing to personal evaluation and commentary:

> Trees are plants,
> Just like flowers.
> I see them in the flower-pots,
> I see them in the bowers,
> I see them in forests,
> I see them in yards.
> But best of all I like
> The daffodils on the hill.
>
> Roses red,
> Pansies all colors,
> Daisies white,
> And all those flowers,
> But best of all
> Are the daffodils
> Sitting on the glowing hill.

Here too we have the child making use of a refrain.

While in the stage of writing the "I like" poems, these children also fall into employing stereotyped phrases. They begin every poem with an identical sequence of words. Some children riot through a series beginning "I like"—as does eight-year-old Fay:

> I like to draw pictures
> And color them too,
> And sometimes I go over the line;
> And then I scribble it.
> And sometimes it is easy,
> And I can do it.
>
> I like the little jelly-fish.
> He's awfully sticky.
> I like to pick them up,
> And then I throw them into the water,
> And then the fishes get them.

She varies the "I like" to a series of "I love":

> I love to write in ink,
> And smear it all over my hands,
> And when it gets too smeary,
> Then I have to use pumice stone—
> What I hate. It's so rough, you know.

Gradually, as has been previously noted, the children relinquish stereotypes in favor of more varied expression. Here is the same child some time after writing the above:

REDWOOD TREE

> Tall, green redwood tree,
> Spreading its great bough over me,
> Patches of blue sky,
> I see as I lie
> On my back at the foot of the tree.

Incidentally this poem shows unusually successful use of rhyme; we will speak of children's use of rhyme in a later chapter.

Other stereotypes begin with "When I . . ." Kathy, eight, dictates:

> When I go on the river,
> When I go through the waves,
> I always think it's a sort of blue cloth
> That spreads over the water.

And

> When I play with chalk,
> It always gets in my nose,
> Mamie always says, "Go wash your face,"
> Or else, "How did that chalk
> Get in your nose?"
> I always have to wash my face anyway.

Stereotypes are so common with young children that any teacher may expect to find his children employing them. He may be inclined to wonder why I have not suggested directing the children's expression into different channels. It seems that anything that serves to induce self-consciousness in the children tends to block their spontaneity, and inasmuch as the children of themselves presently progress to different types of expression there is no reason to make an issue of the matter.

The sevens and eights, like their younger brothers and sisters, dictate what might better be designated stories than poems. Doris writes:

THE LITTLE OLD LADY

Once there was a little old lady.
She was only about twelve years old.
Oh, yes, I mean she was only 1200 years old.
This little old lady thought
She was the youngest person in the world.
She went running about and said,
"I am the youngest person in the world."
And everybody laughed at her. They said,
"You're just the opposite from the youngest,
You're the oldest."
Then she laughed a funny kind of laugh,
And said, "Ho, ho, you think so,
But you're very, very wrong."
And then she went walking down the street proudly,
Laughing and laughing and laughing.
Then she went home and said,
"They don't know anything.
I'm the youngest and not the oldest."
And then she laughed herself to sleep,
And not cried.

Many children begin their poems "Once upon a time," thus indicating their concept of poems as stories. Seven-year-old Mark does not start off with the familiar phrase, but his "Two Pennies" is nonetheless a little story:

I had two pennies.
I went down to a book store.
I asked the man for a book that cost two pennies.
He said, "No! Most certainly not!
It takes paper and ink and typewriters
To make a book.
Wouldn't you think a book would cost more
Than two pennies?"

I said, "Bah!" and went out,
And I went to another book store.
I asked for a book that cost two pennies.
The man said, "Take one."
And I looked around and found a nice little book.
All it had in it was little poems,
But I liked it very much
Because there were pretty little poems,
Like about buttercups and that sort of thing,
And spring times.[2]

It is significant that the book Mark finds is one containing "little poems" which he likes very much.

On the whole the children write fewer "stories" than might be expected. For one thing, they tend to write in short units. Even older children are more at ease in nonexpository writing. One has only to remember the groans with which an assignment of a "composition" is greeted, and the perfunctory and dull performance resulting, to realize that exposition is difficult for children to handle and is distasteful to them. Poetry, dealing as it does with a unit of experience, comes more easily and is more congenial.

Incidentally, short poems receive justification from no less a poet than Edgar Allan Poe, who contended that there is no such thing as a long poem—it is made up only of a sequence of short ones.

In order to suggest to the children that short poems are acceptable, I have frequently read them translations from Japanese poems all of which employ only condensed forms. For the same reason, when the children come to write their own poems, I distribute small paper, six by four inches, so that they are not confronted with a large formidable space that they feel they must fill. The small sheets do not seem to limit them, since when they wish to write more extended poems, they ask for additional paper.

Teachers may be troubled at times by the children's tendency to imitate what they have heard or read. They need not be. Children are natural mimics.. Is not learning to speak in itself largely an act of mimicry? Children are likely to adopt either content or actual expres-

[2] From Flora J. Arnstein, *Children Write Poetry* (New York: Dover Publications, Inc., 1967).

sions from poems they have heard—whole lines in some instances. They do this without compunction, announcing freely, "I got that from"; or another child will comment on someone's poem, "He copied that from. . . ." Cribbing was not always regarded as it is today. Did not Shakespeare appropriate the plots of his plays from whatever sources he chose, and is it not difficult for the listener sometimes to distinguish the early Beethoven from his predecessor, Mozart? So the children may be forgiven behavior sanctioned by their illustrious forbears. It is generally those children who have been early readers or who have read considerably who are inclined to crib. They take over familiar forms, such as the following adopted by Carol, age eight:

> Five pink toes,
> One pink nose—
> That makes a baby.
> Two eyes,
> One mouth,
> That makes a baby.
>
> One neck
> And one baby,
> Makes a baby,
> And an extra neck.[3]

On dictating this, when Carol arrived at the line, "One neck," she stopped, at a loss how to proceed. She shifted from one foot to the other, hesitated a few minutes, then came up triumphantly with the "extra neck." Her solution of her problem, which has convulsed adults to whom the poem has been read, seemed in no way humorous to Carol or to her classmates.

The influence of A. A. Milne is clearly discernable in seven-year-old Kay's

DICTATING

> I'm dictating to my mother,
> I'm dictating to my brother,
> I'm dictating to my sister
> A poem that I read.

[3] From Arnstein, *Ibid.*

I'm dictating to my aunt,
I'm dictating to my uncle,
I'm dictating to my cousin
    A poem that I read.

I'm dictating a poem—
A poem isn't funny,
A poem isn't silly,
A poem is a poem,
    And that is all it is.

It's only just a poem,
It's only just a poem,
It's only just a poem
    A poem that I read.[4]

It is not irrelevant that Kay says she is dictating a poem that she *read*. However, despite the cribbing, the poem indicates that Kay has an innate sense of form—the four-line stanza (with one exception) and the refrain persisting throughout.

At times a child is disturbed by another's "copying" of his poem. In such cases the teacher may observe that nobody can write a completely original poem. Since writing has been going on over the ages, necessarily everything must have already been written about. And one might add that whenever the child who is accused of copying feels he wants to draw on his own ideas he will do so. This reply has seemed to mollify the child who considers himself injured, while it places no stigma on the cribber. It is seldom, though, that children borrow from one another. In cases where they do, it is generally those insecure children who have little confidence in themselves who feel the need to take over another child's ideas. Once faith in themselves has been established, they are only too eager to draw upon their own experience and to explore their own ideas and feelings. Again for the teacher, the indirect approach seems advisable. His continued approval of material that derives from the children's personal experience tends to discourage borrowing and directs the children back to their own sources.

Expressions which the children believe to be "poetic" are apt to appear in poems of beginners. The use of "a" preceding the verb, as "a-sailing,"

[4] From *Ibid.*

and such expressions as "I pray" or "at play" turn up now and again. The observation that people today generally write in the way we speak nowadays seems all that is necessary to direct the children to their natural mode of expression. In any case the use of archaic terms is short-lived. On the whole the teacher will find it desirable to ignore such practices and to allow the children to write whatever comes to them without comment or direction. She may be reassured that many children who start with a very indifferent performance often are able, in the course of the poetry study, to achieve original and delightful writing. Such a one is Carol, who at eight dictates:

> Trees are very useful things:
> Tables, chairs, stools
> And even paper.
> When you see an oak tree
> Standing peacefully in the woods
> You sort of say to yourself,
> "Maybe you'll be turned into a book tomorrow,
> Maybe a fairy-tale will be written on you,
> And maybe you will be turned into
> That particular geography book
> That I hate."

This has little to commend it as a poem, and as an early attempt it gives no indication that this child is to develop into an exceptionally gifted writer.

After a few months' exposure to poetry, however, she writes the following:

> The sea is deep and blue.
> The sea is sometimes green.
> The waves crash on the shore
> Loud as thunder,
> And the clouds above are grey.
>
> The sea gulls must be very cold
> As they sit upon the posts,
> For they quiver and shiver and vibrate.
> Sometimes they are grey,
> And sometimes they are white,
> And they look like the clouds.

The waves with all their white caps
Come clashing into land—
It deafens you.

But when the day is nice,
And the sun shining merrily,
And there are thousands and thousands of sail boats,
The waves are not big at all.
They are not grown up.
It is all so beautiful at sunset,
For the sun makes everything red,
And the sea gulls have a lovely time.
Oh, the sea is beautiful at all times,
Even though the times are very, very different.

Here are shown firsthand observations, a response to different facets of the sea, a smoother cadence, and the use of imagery in the gulls resembling clouds. Of course not all the poems of a child, as is true as well of adults, are of the same quality at any given time, but those of children who have attended poetry classes over a period of years give ample evidence of growth in poetic expression. It can never be assumed what a child may ultimately be able to accomplish; the process of maturing, the exposure to poetry, his ability to gain access to his native resources, and finally the quality of those resources—all will determine what the outcome will be. Nothing grows from nothing, and with the constant exposure to poetry the children unconsciously absorb those characteristics that distinguish it from prose and draw upon these in their own writing.

8

We Come into Poetry

A COMMON PRACTICE in the teaching of music appreciation tends, I believe, to destroy rather than to foster the children's enjoyment of it. Along with the playing of the music, stories of the lives of the composers are presented, with little inconsequential anecdotes concerning them. Notably absent is any commentary on or elucidation of the music itself. The same practice is current in the teaching of poetry. Dates of the poets may be mentioned, their nationality and other factual material concerning them are dwelt upon, but little consideration is given to the poetry as poetry. Content is stressed, but that this content is presented in the context of poetry is ignored. Yet it cannot be dismissed as a matter of no moment that since the writer has employed poetry rather than prose as his medium, there is good reason for discussion of the poetry as poetry.

The same lack of emphasis on poetry as poetry is evidenced by many poetry programs on radio and TV. The discussants concern themselves with the poet's subject matter, his philosophy, his place in history, everything in effect but what constitutes the particular character of his poetry, or what distinguishes it from the poetry of another poet. Reference is seldom made to his individual handling of language, of form, his personal style, or of any other specific attributes of his poetry. While the historical or philosophic approach may have relevance for adults, for the child anything extraneous to the poem itself is irrelevant and misleading. What *is* relevant for the child is the question, "What is this poem saying to me now?" For the younger child it is enough that the poem be related to his understanding, his feeling. But as the children grow older, they are well able to grasp and enjoy those features of poetry that distinguish it as poetry. The shared experience with the poet having already been established, it remains to be recognized that a poem is an experience in itself.

In "Why Poetry?" I mentioned some of the aspects of poetry that the teacher might explore for his own enjoyment. Having done so, he may now share these with his children. At the age of nine or ten some of the children may be ready for an introduction to the elements of poetry, though the age at which these may be presented will be for the teacher to decide. Considerations such as the maturity of his group and whether his children will have been exposed to previous instruction in poetry will enter into his decision.

For example, while a young child will spontaneously employ imagery in a poem of his own writing, he is often unable to entertain the concept of an image. Even in his own poems he sometimes demonstrates confusion with regard to images, as is illustrated by the following poem which John at seven dictates:

THE LITTLE SEA ANIMAL

In the sea the animal roams.
He looks like a horse,
But he does not have eyes,
He does not eat.
He is just foam
That comes up on the sea-shore.
I like to play with the sea horse.
It roars when I get up in the morning,
And also splashes all over me,
So that I should live.
I could not live without the sea horse.
I like to bathe in the sea horse.

Here in likening the foam to a horse, he pushes the analogy beyond reason or sense.

Again in another poem he says, "The wind is blowing just like skirts in the sky," a somewhat more rational use of image though as yet he does not realize its nature. It is as though he senses a need for comparison but has not arrived at the precise concept of an image. When he writes, "The rain looks like water coming down from heaven," he is employing what might be called an abortive image, and this is a form common with beginners. The juxtaposition of two objects not completely dissimilar (since rain *is* water) removes the analogy from the realm of true imagery. The true image compares two disparate objects, heightening the first by underlining the common element in the two. Thus, when a child writes, "A sailboat is like a bird," he is noting the common element in both objects—a certain wing-like structure; it is this common element that performs the function of the image—heightening the picture, giving extension to the meaning.

By the age of ten or thereabouts children are not only able to grasp the concept of image but are avid in identifying these in poems they read. They are ready to discuss the value the particular simile lends to the poems, and they make increasing use of imagery in their own writing. At times certain of my groups have suggested a sort of game—choosing a word and finding images appropriate and applicable to it. On one such occasion Grace, ten, writes:

MOUSE

Tail like a whip,
Size like a door knob,
He sneaks in and out of his hole.[1]

DEER

His antlers like bare trees,
His eyes like hard buttons,
He nibbles the green, green grass.

Louise, eleven, contributes:

GOLD FISH

Darting in and out,
Gold as the sun,
Fast as an arrow,
With fins like the dew in the morning.

Sometimes the children surprise one with outstanding images, as does nine-year-old Joyce:

[1] All five poems from Flora J. Arnstein, *Children Write Poetry* (New York: Dover Publications, Inc., 1967).

BAT

He flies through the night
Like a black surprise . . .

and

TIGER

He leaps through the forest
Like a striped hurricane.

Many an adult poet would have been happy to have created such striking and vivid images as the "black surprise" and the "striped hurricane."

The sound of words in relation to their meaning interests the children greatly. One might read them, as two contrasting uses of "sound" words, the "Noise of Waters," quoted earlier, and "Storm" by "H. D."[2]

STORM

You crash over the trees,
you crack the live branch—
the branch is white,
the green crushed,
each leaf is rent like split wood.

You burden the trees
with black drops,
you swirl and crash—
you have broken off a weighted leaf
in the wind,
it is hurled out,
whirls up and sinks,
a green stone.

In this poem the children enjoy identifying the words that express action by their sound, such as *clash, crash*, and also those words or phrases that are "picture-making."[3]

[2] From H. D., *Sea Garden* (London: Constable, 1916).
[3] See "The Teacher's Dilemma," p. 8.

Older children are responsive to the symbolic content of a poem. Matthew indicates this readiness at twelve when he says, "I like poems that mean more than they mean." "The Road Not Taken" by Robert Frost provides an example of the symbolic in poetry.

It might be helpful at this point to illustrate one of the many possible presentations of this poem. Just as it has been suggested earlier with reference to the younger children that the children's own experience be explored before reading a poem, so with the upper elementary children, before reading the poem, the setting or the general idea of the poem should be touched upon. There need be no extended exposition of the poem's content, just enough so that the children are enabled to orient themselves to it. "The Road Not Taken" might be summarized in this fashion: "This poem deals with the experience of walking in a wood and arriving at a spot where two roads diverge or separate. The poet chooses one of the roads." If possible the poem might be written on the blackboard since it might be difficult to deal with it analytically only by hearing it—we are all today to some extent "eye-minded."

THE ROAD NOT TAKEN

Two roads diverged in a yellow wood,
And sorry I could not travel both
And be one traveler, long I stood
And looked down one as far as I could
To where it bent in the undergrowth;

Then took the other, as just as fair,
And having perhaps the better claim,
Because it was grassy and wanted wear;
Though as for that the passing there
Had worn them really about the same,

And both that morning equally lay
In leaves no step had trodden black.
Oh, I kept the first for another day!
Yet knowing how way leads on to way,
I doubted if I should ever come back.

I shall be telling this with a sigh
Somewhere ages and ages hence:
Two roads diverged in a wood, and I—
I took the road less traveled by,
And that has made all the difference.[4]

One might begin by taking up the content of the poem. Questions might be asked: What road did the poet take and why? What does his choice tell you about the man? What is the implication of the title? Such questions lead directly to the matter of symbolic interpretation. Is the poet speaking exclusively about a road? Or it might be asked, if the children have not already brought the matter up, is the poet saying anything about the making of choices? And this in turn might lead to a discussion of the universal predicament of choice and where this leads.

But, as I mentioned earlier, one must not be restricted to dealing with the content of a poem alone, or as a matter of fact with any one aspect of a poem to the exclusion of others. A young teacher told me of the tendency of her group while in teacher training to embark on what she called "a safari of image hunting," to the point where they became so obsessed with this exercise that their interest was limited solely to this one phase of poetry.

With relation to the poem noted above the question might be posed, why should this subject be presented in poetic form? Someone might come up with the remark, perhaps not entirely innocent of the intent to disconcert the teacher, that it is written in poetry because the writer was a poet. If the idea was to slightly discomfort the teacher, it miscarries with his reply, "Precisely. But what does the presentation as poetry do for the subject that prose might not have done equally well?" In order to bring out one point he might ask each member of the class to write in prose the content of the first three lines, through the word "traveler." Such a prose rendering might read: "I was walking along a road in a wood to where the road separated into two forks. I was sorry I could not take both forks, but being only one person I could not do so." Now the class might be asked to count the words in the poetic version—they add up to eighteen—then to count those in their prose version. In mine they add up to thirty-six.

[4] From Robert Frost, *Complete Poems of Robert Frost* (New York: Holt, Rinehart and Winston, 1949).

The difference between the number of words necessary to express the same thought in poetry and prose brings up another aspect of poetry: that of condensation, compression. Poetry expresses by a sort of shorthand, by suggestion, or by other means what it is not possible to express in the same space in prose. And, as any condensation leads to tension, so too a subject gains a certain dynamic quality by the tension inherent in poetic rendering. (Of course one need not express the matter in these terms to children.) They may be shown, for example, how much is implied by the final line: "And that has made all the difference." In these seven simple words are suggested the idea of how a person's whole life may be changed in the moment of a single choice. And one may note the understatement, as again expressed in, "I shall be telling this with a sigh." How much emotion is conveyed and how much of recollection and regret are carried by the phrase, "Somewhere ages and ages hence"! Content and condensation, however, do not exhaust the matter for discussion offered by this poem. They have been presented here merely as examples of the varied approaches which may bring to the children aspects of poetry that will be new to them.

Condensation is also illustrated through the poetry of the Japanese. The forms employed, the *hokku* and the *tanka*, the first consisting of only seventeen syllables, the last, thirty-one, are telling examples of how much may be suggested by restricted means. One may speculate that for the Japanese the short poem serves to stimulate the imagination to carry the thought onward. One might compare the effect with that of a pebble thrown in a lake, the concentric circles expanding wider and wider; just so the thought is carried on beyond what is said to the limits of the readers' imaginative powers.

I append a couple of examples since I employ these and similar poems in my work with the children.

> O Pine-Tree
> At the side of the stone house,
> When I look at you,
> It is like seeing face to face
> With men of old time.[5]

[5] All these Japanese poems are from Elias Lieberman (editor), *Poems for Enjoyment* (New York: McGraw-Hill, 1931).

This poem by "The Priest Hakatsu," translated by Arthur Waley, by its delicate suggestion stimulates one's thoughts to the recollection of the old days and then men living then. The past is brought to the present by the confrontation "face to face" with the living pine trees (associated with the old men), whose ridges are of today and yet have been made by the passing years.

Similar imaginative evocation occurs in the following two poems:

> My heart thinking
> "How beautiful he is"
> Is like a swift river
> Which though one dams it and dams it,
> Will still break through.

This, by "The Lady of Sakanoye," is rendered in English by the same translator. Another poet, Okura, is translated by Mabel Lorenz:

THE MOUNTAIN TOP

> Because the plum trees on the peak
> Are up so high,
> The buzz of bees about their bloom
> Comes from the sky!

Poems such as these allow the child a congenial play of imagination and lead him to search behind the literal facades for further meanings. And such reading-with-the-imagination is especially to be cultivated in connection with poetry.

Here a word may be interpolated concerning the teacher's response to the children's comments. These are bound to be in many cases immature and irrelevant, or may even contain false inferences, but whatever their nature, they should be accorded respectful reception. Nor need the teacher acclaim any "correct' or particularly significant remark; by doing so he will be diverting the children's concern from the matter under discussion to that of offering observations that presumably will gain his approval. To single out any one child for special commendation is as undesirable as to single him out for condemnation. Response is to be encouraged, and the quality of the response will improve through continued exposure to poetry.

Suggestion, in addition to explicit exposition, whether with condensation or not, occurs in English poetry as well as in Japanese. "The Listeners" by Walter de la Mare lends itself admirably as an example. The children's interest is immediately aroused by the poet's having placed the reader squarely in the middle of his story without any hint of the incidents leading up to the climax, or elucidating to what commitment the traveler is referring. Searching for interpretations and trying to envisage possible situations that might have given rise to the incident described offer an imaginative challenge to the children's inventiveness.

THE LISTENERS

"Is there anybody there?" said the Traveller,
    Knocking at the moonlit door;
And his horse in the silence champed the grasses
    Of the forest's ferny floor:
And a bird flew up out of the turret,
    Above the Traveller's head:
And he smote upon the door again a second time;
    "Is there anybody there?" he said.
But no one descended to the Traveller;
    No head from the leaf-fringed sill
Leaned over and looked into his grey eyes,
    Where he stood perplexed and still.
But only a host of phantom listeners
    That dwelt in the lone house then
Stood listening in the quiet of the moonlight
    To the voice from the world of men:
Stood thronging the faint moonbeams on the dark stair,
    That goes down to the empty hall,
Harkening in the air stirred and shaken
    By the lonely Traveller's call.
And he felt in his heart their strangeness,
    Their stillness answering his cry,
While his horse moved, cropping the dark turf,
    'Neath the starred and leafy sky;
For he suddenly smote on the door, even
    Louder, and lifted his head:—
"Tell them I came, and no one answered,
    That I kept my word," he said.

Never the least stir made the listeners,
    Though every word he spake
Fell echoing through the shadowiness of the still house
    From the one man left awake:
Ay, they heard his foot upon the stirrup,
    And the sound of iron on stone,
And how the silence surged softly backward,
    When the plunging hoofs were gone.[6]

The poem lends itself to a wealth of poetic discovery. One feature that has not been previously mentioned is that of the music inherent in poetry. Reading this poem aloud, one becomes more aware of the music of the lines, the smoothness of their flow, and harking back to the "Noise of Waters" quoted in "Why Poetry?" one can note here a similar cadential quality.

The mood evoked by the poem can also be explored, notably the passage from "the host of phantom listeners" through to the "Traveller's call." The "faint moonbeams," the "dark stair," the "empty hall," the "air stirred and shaken"—all these phrases are calculated to arouse the feeling of eeriness, of strangeness. And attention might be drawn to the exactness of description of hoofbeats as "the sound of iron on stone," and how this is another telling example of condensation—the sound of the horse galloping away suggested merely by the "iron on stone." The contrast in the following line might be noted, as the poet resumes the mood of strangeness by the words "the silence surged softly backward" with their "S" sounds (like the admonition "Sh") reinforcing the idea of silence. I have made a point of calling to the children's notice the feeling a poem gives one, since children are sensitive to feeling, and attention drawn to it brings the realization that poetry is directed to the emotions as well as to the mind. It is obvious that not every poem lends itself to evaluation in terms of feeling.

Repetition of lines and the use of refrain open up another area of interest. The children might be asked, for example, what does the poet intend to convey by the repetition of the final line in each stanza of "The Pasture"? What function does the repetition of the last two lines of each stanza in "The Shepherdess" perform? Again, in the poem "Recuerdo" by Edna St. Vincent Millay, what does the repeated "We

[6] From Walter de la Mare, *The Listeners* (New York: Holt, Rinehart and Winston, undated).

were very ~~happy~~ *tired*, we were very merry" do for the poem? Or Robert Frost's repetition of "And miles to go before I sleep" in his "Stopping by Woods on a Snowy Evening"?

In the next poem quoted there is a novel use of repetition which the children will be interested in discovering. One might explore the use of refrain in the old ballads—and speaking of ballads, a wealth of material here in both the old and new will delight the children. Such comparatively modern ballads as "The Highwayman" by Alfred Noyes and "The Inchcape Rock" never fail in appeal. It will interest the children likewise to be made aware of the condensation employed in the ballads—how much of the story is told by implication or by snatches of conversation.

We may now turn to the consideration of rhythm in poetry which I have delayed discussing because it, and rhyme, are too often treated as the only components of poetry. Let us begin by having the children clap the number of beats (the stressed syllables) in the following poem by James Stephens:

THE SNARE

I hear a sudden cry of pain!
    There is a rabbit in a snare;
Now I hear the cry again,
    But I cannot tell from where.

But I cannot tell from where
    He is calling out for aid;
Crying on the frightened air,
    Making everything afraid.

Making everything afraid,
    Wrinkling up his little face,
And he cries again for aid;
    And I cannot find the place!

And I cannot find the place
    Where his paw is in the snare;
Little one! Oh, little one!
    I am searching everywhere.[7]

[7] From James Stephens, *Collected Poems of James Stephens* (New York: Macmillan, rev. ed., 1954).

We find here consistent lines of four beats each. Looking back at "The Shepherdess," we find lines of four beats alternating with lines of three. In "The Pasture" we have two stanzas with the first three lines containing five beats and the fourth containing, roughly speaking, four, though practically every word is stressed. Countless variations of rhythm occur in poetry, and the children, once they are introduced to the possible variations, eagerly pursue their own discoveries in this field.

I would not suggest any more extensive analysis of meter with children, but the teacher might be interested in examining further subtleties of rhythm. Clapping the rhythm of the first stanza of "The Snare," we get the following general pattern of stressed (−) syllables and unstressed (◡):

$$\breve{} - \breve{} - \breve{} - \breve{} -$$
I hear a sud/den cry/ of pain!

$$\breve{} \; - \breve{} - \; \breve{} - \breve{} \; -$$
There is/a rab/bit in/a snare;

$$- \quad \breve{} - \quad \breve{} - \quad \breve{} -$$
Now/ I hear/ the cry/ again,

$$- \quad \breve{} - \quad \breve{} - \quad \breve{} \quad -$$
But/ I can/not tell/ from where.

The basic pattern then, is unstress-stress (the iambic which is employed in the bulk of English poetry). The pattern of four beats to a line, however, is not affected by the omitted unstress at the beginning of the last two lines. Examining the lines more carefully and reading the words as they would be accented in speech, we find that we give a sort of intermediate accent, for example, on the word "I" and "Now." Using the symbol of ″ for this intermediate accent, we find the verse gives us the following pattern:

$$″ \; - \breve{} - \; \breve{} - \; \breve{} \; -$$
I hear/ a sud/den cry/ of pain!

$$\breve{} \; \breve{}\breve{} \; - \breve{} \; \breve{}\breve{} \; -$$
There is a/ rabbit/ in a snare;

$$″ \; ″ \; - \quad \breve{} - \; \breve{} -$$
Now I hear/ the cry/ again

$$\breve{} \; ″ \; - \; \breve{} - \; \breve{} \quad -$$
But I can/not tell/ from where.

The pattern, now, instead of being the consistent ∪ — of our clapped verse, becomes a very different and more complicated rhythm.

$$″ - / ∪ - / ∪ - / ∪ -$$
$$∪ ∪ ∪ / \_ ∪ / ∪ ∪ -$$
$$″ ″ - / ∪ - / ∪ -$$
$$∪ ″ - / ∪ - / ∪ -$$

However one may divide the beats into units (and there might be different ways of doing this), the pattern is notably different from the clapped one. Thus within any all-over fixed pattern there may be innumerable variations. This interplay of the natural stress of words against the basic rhythm—a sort of counterpoint—adds immeasurably to the interest of the rhythm, and the reader senses this interplay even if he is not consciously aware of it. The presence of this counterpoint is an added reason for a poem not to be read with the jingly rhythm common with some readers.

Another type of rhythmic variation may be of interest. In a stanza from a poem by Edna St. Vincent Millay, "Travel," we find the lines:

> The railroad track is miles away,
> And the day is loud with voices speaking,
> Yet there isn't a train goes by all day
> But I hear its whistle shrieking.[8]

This, too, has the basic iambic rhythm, but note lines two and four. Here, instead of starting with one unstressed syllable, the poet starts with two: And the day, Yet there isn't, and such additions of extra syllables may occur at any point in a line—as, for example, it does in the third line: isn't a train. Another variation is the "feminine" ending of a line, with an unstressed final syllable as in speaking, and shrieking.

Departures from basic patterns add life and interest to rhythm. Should the rhythmic stress coincide consistently with the word stress, or if there were no occasional additions of syllables to vary the basic beat, the lines would be of an intolerable monotony.

[8] From Edna St. Vincent Millay, *Collected Poems* (New York: Harper & Row, 1956).

The many possible variations of rhythm are of continuing interest to children. Here is an amusing free use of rhythm in the following poem by Hilaire Belloc.

TARANTELLA

Do you remember an Inn,
  Miranda?
Do you remember an Inn?
And the tedding and the spreading
Of the straw for a bedding,
And the fleas that tease in the High Pyrenees,
And the wine that tasted of the tar?
And the cheers and the jeers of the young muleteers
(Under the vine of the dark verandah)—
Do you remember an Inn, Miranda?
Do you remember an Inn?
And the cheers and the jeers of the young muleteers
Who hadn't got a penny,
And who weren't paying any,
And the hammer at the doors and the din?
And the Hip, Hop, Hap!
Of the clap
Of the hands to the twirl and the swirl
Of the girl gone chancing,
Glancing,
Dancing,
Backing and advancing,
Snapping of the clapper to the spin
Out and in—
And the ting, tong, tang of the Guitar!
Do you remember an Inn, Miranda?
Do you remember an Inn?

Never more, Miranda;
Never more.
Only the high peaks hoar;
And Aragon torrent at the door.
No sound
In the walls of the Halls where falls
The tread

Of the feet of the dead to the ground.
No sound:
But the boom
Of the far Waterfall like Doom.[9]

In this poem there is no commitment to regularity of rhythm. The beginning gives the effect of a wild dance, with its short single-syllabled words, together with the skillful juxtaposition of two-syllabled and the short vowel sounds contrasted with the long (short "i's" in *Inn*, short "e's" in *tedding*, as against the long "e's" in *fleas*, and the long "i's" in *wine*). The internal rhyme, *cheers, jeers*, rhyming with mule*teers*, also adds to the speed, the dancelike quality of the verse. Notice also how the poet alters the mood in the last stanza, passing from the jingling words, *tedding, spreading*, the short crisp ones such as *clap, snap*, to a sequence of words containing long vowel sounds, as in *more, hoar, door, ground, sound*—all reinforcing the idea that the old happy times are now gone. With the opening words "never more" we are immediately introduced to the somber present whose mood culminates in the final lines "Only the boom/ Of the far Waterfall like Doom."

The use of rhyme may be studied with the children. With the letters of the alphabet as symbols, the rhyme scheme of "The Snare" is charted:

> pain—a
> snare—b
> again—a
> where—b

and so on. In "The Shepherdess" the rhyme scheme is

> delight—a
> sheep—b
> white—a
> steep—b
> height—a
> sleep—b

In "The Pasture" we have a, b, b, c, for the first stanza and d, e, e, c for the second. All the possible variations of rhyme will be of interest to

[9] From Blanche Jennings Thompson (editor), *More Silver Pennies* (New York: Macmillan, 1939).

the children—the regular and the irregular, as illustrated in "Tarantella." A stimulating discussion would result from the question why rhyme is employed and what function it serves in a poem.

Here, then, summarized, are some of the elements of poetry that may be brought to the children's notice: imagery, symbolism, mood, repetition, condensation, suggestion, alliteration, rhyme, and rhythm. By the time the children have been introduced to all of these they will be able to respond to poetry with an enthusiastic awareness that will challenge and delight the teacher. And with this freshness of vision and enhanced perception of poetry will come evaluation and appreciation that will not be restricted to poetry alone but that will extend the children's general outlook and bring a new enrichment to their lives.

9

We Write to Learn

Tom comes to my desk when the poetry writing is in progress. He is obviously troubled. "I can't think of anything to write about," he says. In any teacher's group whenever writing is in progress there will occasionally be found several such Tom's, and this is not to be wondered at. Having been assigned specific topics to write on during his school life, Tom is naturally overwhelmed when the whole world of subject matter is open to him to choose from. What can be done to help him? We might embark on a private conference in which we talk about things that interest him, his hobbies, how he spends his free time. Before long, Tom's face kindles and he says, "Oh, I know! I can write about . . ." such and such. Tom is now on his own. He knows where to turn for his material. Where else should this be than to himself and what interests him? For the teacher to suggest subject matter would be to direct him away from his creative self which alone is the source of his authentic impulsion. I have tried both suggesting subject matter and allowing the children to choose their own, but I have found that it is wiser to direct the child to his inherent creative sources. It may be more difficult in the beginning to lead some children to tap their own resources, but in the long run it is the most rewarding—since they do better work when "sparked" from within than from without.

Jane is less articulate. She doesn't come to my desk. She sits, pencil in hand, observing her classmates absorbed in composition, and slinks past me when the period is over. Jane really wants to write. We find that out when she and I talk. With her it is not a question of not knowing what to write but of not knowing how to get started. And this, too, is not surprising. How does one have the courage to express one's thoughts and feelings? How does one dare to expose oneself to criticism or perhaps even ridicule? Many young people grow wary as they grow

73

older, and with wariness unfortunately comes the possibility of loss of
access to their deeper selves. Jane needs, above all, reassurance. "You
don't *have* to write," I tell her. "Write only when, and if, you feel like
doing so." And I add the further reassurance, "Anything you write
that you don't want read aloud, just tell me and I won't read it." With
the pressure off, Jane also finds reassurance in the fact that none of the
poems handed in are either corrected or criticized. All, she notes, are
met with acceptance, none singled out for acclaim, none rejected as
inadequate. Jane comes to feel that the teacher's attitude toward writing is in no way different from that which he assumes toward work
in any other field, arithmetic or spelling; no more is made of it. This
realization is often all that is necessary to enable the timid child to
take her first step and, once launched, to go forward without fear.

Often creative work seems to some people to call for a sort of special
consideration—as though the mere fact of writing a poem casts some sort
of aura around the activity. If the teacher does not overweight the writing, the children are relieved of certain fears surrounding it.

Though the teacher may place no pressure on the children's writing,
and though they may interpret his attitude as one of not being over-
concerned with it, they are far from undervaluing the experience themselves. The feeling already quoted of the boy who said, "Writing is
the best part of it [the poetry session]," is corroborated by the behavior of the many children who have cherished poems of their own
writing over the years. The children have made small looseleaf binders
in which to collect their poems; these have proved an additional incentive to writing, in that both in anticipation and in the accumulation of a
volume of one's own poems resides an additional satisfaction. There is
value in having such a compilation available—the children not only
enjoy rereading their earlier efforts, but they are often able to chart
progress and achieve a sense of accomplishment. In a large class the
teacher cannot, of course, type the children's poems as I did, but small
notebooks may be provided in which the children may copy their own
poems, after these have been corrected for spelling, punctuation, line
spacing, or for any flagrant errors in grammar. This type of correction
is unlike the correction of the poems themselves, which I do not
sanction. Though the poetry sessions should not be made the occasion
for the teaching of spelling, punctuation, etc., there is no reason why
the mistakes should be perpetuated.

Any corrections other than these seem inadvisable, since, as I have said earlier, no specific "rights" and "wrongs" may be applied to creative writing. What a child writes at any given time is valid as an expression of his development at that particular stage. Teachers are constantly asking, "How are children to improve if they aren't given specific instruction?" They *do* improve, and any doubts on that score I believe will be allayed when we turn our attention later to the children's development in poetic criteria. In my opinion the most fruitful method of teaching in the field of creative writing is one of indirection. The constant reading of poetry, with attention drawn to felicities of expression, to the poetic practices described in the last chapter, brings to the child the sense of what constitutes poetry. And though this sense is in the main unconscious, it is nonetheless valuable; in fact, perhaps because it is unconscious it is the more operative in the writing. Does not what we call "inspiration" derive largely from the so-called unconscious? We pay verbal tribute even if we do not actually acknowledge this fact when we say of something we have written, "It just came to me."

From the behavior of the Tom's and the Jane's, the teacher will discover that it is not so easy to initiate writing with the older as with the younger children. Many things have happened to a child in the process of growing older that may tend to inhibit freedom of expression. Not the least of these is self-consciousness. Assurance of acceptance is even more essential to the older than to the younger child, since the former is more inclined to be critical of his own performance. Often this criticism is not valid on poetic grounds. It may grow primarily out of the child's lack of confidence in himself. He forestalls the criticism of others by asserting, in advance, "It's no good." Here is an example of faulty evaluation in a poem written by twelve-year-old Prue:

WINDOWS

There is a house on the hill that has many windows:
Windows in the cellar, windows in the garret,
Windows everywhere.
Some look cross and frowning
As if they dared anyone to look inside them.
Some look inviting, some happy, some sad.
One bay window looks out haughty and proud,
And a tiny attic window, like a smiling child.

The windows on the first floor are very slim,
Tall and beautiful, but they look as though they had
   no feeling.
The windows in one of the bedrooms
Look from behind some lacy curtains,
As if smiling knowingly
To remember the good times they have seen.
The windows of the big bedroom look imposing,
Not deigning to notice the others.
Every time I go by the house, I nod to the windows.
I feel that I know them,
That they are old friends.[1]

This is a poem no twelve-year-old need be ashamed of, and yet after writing it, Prue crumpled it and threw it in the waste basket. When I asked to see it, she gave the usual reply, "It's no good." But after I had told her that sometimes even an adult poet is not able to decide immediately after the writing whether a poem is good, and when I assured her that I would show it to no one, she overcame her reluctance and handed it to me. Later, as evidence of her growth in self-confidence, she submitted it to the school magazine, where it was accepted. Should she have discarded it, she would in all probability have felt discouraged and have discontinued writing, with a consequent loss to herself of a significant experience.

An added difficulty for the older child results from his having built up preconceptions of poetry that the younger child has not as yet acquired. Thinking, as he generally does, of poetry in terms of rhythm and rhyme, he is often fearful of attempting what seems to him a difficult undertaking. And in these terms it *is* difficult. To acquire a technique in the handling of rhythm and rhyme is an arduous task and obligatory only on those who are dedicated to becoming poets. Since our objective in the poetry study is not to make poets of our young people, but rather to open up the field of poetry to them, it would seem wiser to suggest that in their writing they avail themselves of the latitude of free verse. Having been introduced to free verse through our reading, the children feel this to be a legitimate form of poetry. They realize in addition that they are better able to express their thoughts

---

[1] From Flora J. Arnstein, *Children Write Poetry* (New York: Dover Publications, Inc., 1967).

and feelings in this medium than when constricted by the exigencies
of meter and rhyme. The attempt to force their thoughts into strict
forms obliges them to abandon their initial ideas or so manipulate them
that they lose authenticity. A poem such as the following illustrates
into what banalities the commitment to rhythm and rhyme drives the
child:

DULL DAY

On a dreary, dreary morning,
A dull, dull day,
As I sat at my window,
Sleeping the day away,
My cat was lying and mewing,
Just as if to say,
"If you have nothing to do,
Please pet me, I pray."[2]

What does this poem say that derives from a child's observation and
feeling? Note the obsolete expression, "I pray." Strangely enough, the
children often fall into such archaic usages (the *a-sailing, a-riding* noted
earlier) when writing in metrical form.

In distinction to the above poem, here are poems by the same child,
when after a prolonged addiction to trite rhythmic verse, she finally
abandons it in favor of free verse. At nine she writes:

THE OCEAN FROM DIFFERENT POINTS OF VIEW

1

O mighty ocean,
O roaring waves, and banks of foam,
How can we, small and feeble as we are,
Plunge into your depths unafraid?

2

O scaly, shiny dragon,
How can the waves break through your hard coat
To make the little ripples in the water?

[2] From Arnstein, *Ibid.*

3

What are you chasing,
Ocean, great ocean,
That you rush upon the shore
Only to fall back again discouraged, fatigued?

At ten she writes:

WEATHER

A warm murkiness is hanging on the air.
Every once in a while it rains in little torrents,
And then it stops.
The sky cannot make up its mind what to do,
So it just lets the clouds play tag with the sun.

Here, in these poems, we find accurate observation, individual reactions, imagery, and a general play of imagination totally lacking in her rhythmic poems.

One eight-year-old writes in meter and rhyme:

Down by the brook in the middle of spring,
I look around and things seem to sing.
Around the brook are little flowers,
And up above there are no towers.

Aside from the absurdity of the towers, introduced solely for the rhyme, we have here the absence of specificity in the "things" that seem to sing. Ineptitudes such as these occur constantly in the children's rhymed and rhythmic poems.

In contrast the same little girl writes the following at a later poetry session:

THE CLOUDS

In the daytime
Sometimes the clouds blot out the sun.
Sometimes they are all different colors,
Like reddish pink, light pink,
And like blue, lavender,
Purple and green.

Sometimes they are big grey clouds
Floating in the sky.
Sometimes they look like popcorn,
Or little lost sheep in a valley.

In the night time
Sometimes they are white.
Then they look very pretty.
Sometimes they blot out the stars,
So you can't see the stars at all.
But I like the clouds in the day time
Best of all.

Here we have the real child, expressing herself in accordance with her age (note the enumeration and the phrase "I like") and giving evidence of personal observation in such comparisons as the clouds to popcorn and the charming resemblance to "little lost sheep in a valley."

She turns to consideration of herself in the following:

ME

Me is always me
When I look at myself in the mirror
It is me.
I am always me.
The "Me" in me never goes away.
I am always here—
Me and myself.

The question of identity which preoccupies many writers of today is here invoked by a child of eight! One is continually surprised by the children's concern with areas that we tend to think the exclusive province of adults.

Carol provides a prime example of the crippling effect of the attempt to adopt metric forms.[3] She is a particularly gifted child and at the age of ten is able to handle rhythm and rhyme with a certain dexterity. The following poem is an illustration:

[3] See *Ibid.*, page 30, for a more extended examination of this child's writing.

And through the willow leaves,
Behind the birches' white bark,
Far beyond the ferns and grasses,
The river flows on dark.

And in the happy sunlight,
Beyond the grey rocks' way,
Among the reeds and rushes,
The sparkling brooklet lay.

And in the gurgling fountain,
In lovely gardens of kings,
Making the grass wet and dewy,
The brook flies on without wings.

Slipping down from ridges,
Rushing into the lane,
It joins the mighty river
Swollen large with rain.

In essence this poem says nothing, though it indicates that this child has read some poetry and has achieved a glib command of language. It is full of irrelevance—such as the garden of kings, and the brook rushing down a *lane*; it contains a change of tense from the present used throughout in order to supply a rhyme for "way."

Contrast it with the following poems written later:

Golden trumpets of the spring,
Announcing the day—
The daffodils are breathing.
Are breathing away the winter.
Quivering to the wind—
The spring daffodils.

. . . .

On a low hill
Lit by the moon.
A row of young pine trees
Stood silhouetted against the night.

. . . .

The tide-line is on the shore now.
It is where the ocean puts its ripples to dry,
And stores its freshness.

> It's where the ocean puts the sprouting onions,
> And heaps the brown sea-weeds.
> They look like dead lions
> Scattered on the sand.

While likening the daffodils to trumpets is not an original observation,[4] the statement that they are "breathing away the winter" is a delightful concept. Also the picture of young pine trees silhouetted against the night arises from authentic observation. And the ocean putting its ripples to dry on the tide-line is an amusing imaginative touch. At twelve Carol has travelled from the literal into the realm of suggestion, as she well knows by entitling this poem "Impressionistic":

> I went one night to where the marshes meet the moon,
> To where the last oak of the world stands alone.

All the free verse here quoted, whatever its limitation as written by children, is still imbued with the genuine stuff of which poetry is made —with personal commentary and imaginative evocation. And the same is never true when the children employ metrical forms, for in such practice they invariably lose touch with their subjective world. Since the world of their thoughts and feelings is alone meaningful and of value to them, inasmuch as it is the source of whatever creative impulses they may have, it would seem wise to direct them to it, and, without being insistent, suggest they avail themselves of free verse rather than metrical as being better adapted to their expression.

But we have anticipated ourselves. A question teachers most frequently ask is, "How do you get the writing started?" Often merely the remark, "How would you like to try your hand at writing?" is all that is necessary to get the children under way. Another incentive grew out of the fact that previously the children had made the looseleaf booklets in which to keep their original poems. As I mentioned earlier, I would type the poems written at each session and return these at the

---

[4] This simile is of course not original to adults, but it may be to a child. This, however, involves no problem, since no comment is made to the child on the quality of the simile. While it is true that much that might be trite to an adult is new to a child, it is equally true that children's observations are rarely trite. They do see things freshly, and many an adult poet envies the fresh vision of the child.

following, when the children would enter them in their books. During the term the poems were held in place by brass clips which were replaced at the end of the year by permanent cords.

Reading the poems written by other children, such as those of Hilda Conkling, also stimulates the desire to write, as do those contained in my book *Children Write Poetry* or in *Creative Youth* by Hughes Mearns.[5] Actually the launching of the writing is easier than teachers anticipate. But assuring the continuance of writing is more difficult. Many teachers, not only of children but also of college students, have observed that the impulse to write is inclined to flag after a time. This need not happen. Given the room climate already outlined, and the teacher's acceptance, the children continue, I have found, to write indefinitely.

There are, however, certain pitfalls which the teacher may fall into that lead to discontinuance of writing. Perhaps my experience in having fallen into these has brought me a certain awareness which may be of help to other teachers in avoiding them. One that contributed to unfortunate results for a child was my not having apprised the parents in advance of the nature of the creative writing program. Parents are naturally, and in some cases justifiably, proud of the achievements of their offspring, but in certain instances the expression of such pride is likely to place barriers in the way of the child. Matthew, aged twelve, instead of handing in his poem at the end of the writing session asked, "Would it be all right if I take my poem home first to show to my mother?" Not foreseeing any unfavorable consequences, I made no objection. Here is the poem:

NEWS

A click-click-click,
Half a hundred typewriters pounding,
Like the music of a machine gun.
They crash, they pound,
And then one breaks.
All the typewriters pounding,
Pounding out news for the press—
Bad news, good news, tabloid news
All for the daily press.

[5] (New York: Dover Publications, 1959.)

In the next building is a telegraph office,
With the steady dot-dash, dot-dash of the telegraph equipment,
Echoing, re-echoing through the building,
Sending news all over the world—
Bad news, good news, important news,
Sent over the whole world.

Down the street a telephone office,
With its honeycomb of little holes,
With little plugs to match—
A myriad of little buttons,
Plugs, switches, and electrical connections,
A network of wires running in and out,
And a steady, running buzz of conversation,
Conversation everywhere,
Sent everywhere,
Received everywhere—
A telephone office is a busy thing.

News, news being sent everywhere,
To all parts of the world—
News of business failures, business successes,
News of death, news of sickness,
News of joy, news of happiness . . .
What would you, what could you do
Without news?[6]

This is a very acceptable piece of work, especially as an early attempt. But Matthew's mother was so impressed by it that she read it to a friend who was in some way connected with publishing and who suggested the poem's publication. Matthew's mother arrived at school the next day to discuss the matter. I advised her against taking such a step, but unfortunately the damage had already been done to Matthew. He had been made to feel he had accomplished something especially noteworthy, and as a result he became self-conscious about his writing. Whether he was wondering before embarking on a new poem if it would "be as good as 'News'," or whether in the writing the same idea obtruded, there was no knowing. In any event a long time elapsed before

[6] From Arnstein, *op. cit.*

he could write spontaneously again. His subsequent poems were stilted and wooden. Overpraise, strangely enough, seems to block a child's creativity, and this is an additional reason for the teacher to accept the child's poem in a casual manner.

A conference with the parents of individual children ahead of time or some general talk with the parents of the class, in which the teacher outlines the aim of creative writing, would have obviated such an incident as the above and insured the children's continuance of writing. In my later classes, until such a conference had been held, I did not permit the children to take their poems home.

Another unfortunate situation might have been avoided if I had followed this last procedure. Irene, a member of an after-school high school group that met with me informally for two years, wrote the following poem:

FLY

O Fly,
Climbing glass panes,
Why not go out
When I open the window?
Are *we* all like that?

O Fly,
The air outside's free.
Beautiful air—
(Just a bit lower, Fly,)
What's wrong, Fly,
Can't you see?
Are *we* like that?

O Fly,
Struggling desperately,
Mastering the slippery false glass,
You only fall back bruised.
Are *we* like that?

O Fly,
What is glass?
A delusion and a snare
With no meaning for you,

Or a big thing
With a meaning
Great as the world?

O Fly,
Are we comrades,
You and I?
Of what good are you,
Or I?
Are we all like that?

O Fly,
Climbing glass panes,
It's time you *knew* that glass is glass!
Learn then, O Fly.
But you won't.
I won't.
The world won't.
O Fly,
We are all like that—
We are comrades, O Fly,
You and I.[7]

I think we can agree that this poem gives indication of a native gift
for expression and a marked feeling for form, for structure, and for
climax. Had this girl, along with being exposed to poetry, continued
to write, she would, in my opinion, have undoubtedly developed a sense
of cadence and a generally more poetic mode of expression. But what
happened was that Irene was eager to take her poem home to show her
father. A close relationship existed between the two, and his approval
was meaningful to her. But he did not approve. "It's no poem," he told
her. "It has no rhythm and no rhyme." Irene had nothing at her command with which to counter this verdict and came to class next week
crestfallen. The fact that her father, as she admitted, never read poetry
did not seem to affect her acceptance of his dictum. I reminded her of
the Psalms we had read, of Carl Sandburg and of Walt Whitman, and
she regained enough confidence to submit the poem a short time later
to her school paper. But here again she met rebuff. The teacher who

[7] From *Ibid.*

passed upon contributions rejected the poem on the same grounds as her father. The combined repudiation was apparently too much for Irene. She never attempted to write again. Perhaps I should have been skillful enough to have helped her overcome her discouragement, but sometimes discouragement strikes so deeply that all attempts to surmount it are unavailing.

Criticism seems to strike at the very root of the creative impulse. Even in the case of adults, I have observed that ill-advised criticism has often resulted in such bewilderment as to inhibit writing. Only the rarest and most skillful teacher and one with long experience in the creative field can offer fruitful criticism, and, what is of as great importance, know the correct time to tender it. But for the child, criticism is invariably fatal to writing. Aside from making for self-consciousness, that prime deterrent to creation, it leads to confusion which has a like result. For criticism means the application of adult standards to the work of a child, and a child is not ready for such standards. Preoccupation with them induces in him the concern, "Is this correct or all right?" And this concern should not be forced upon him. He should be permitted to write and write, untrammeled by any outside considerations. Only by continuous writing will he learn, as the title of this chapter states: "We Write to Learn," which some readers may have taken for a misprint, thinking it should read "We Learn to Write." But the wording was advised, for nowhere is the old precept of learning by doing more applicable than to the writing of poetry.

We err in lack of faith in the child. In a skill such as skating, a child learns propulsion and balance by himself, by means of trial and error. Just so will he learn in writing. Only when he has had continuous access to his creative sources and has had a long experience of writing should he be concerned with the application of standards. And these standards will then be his own. They will have been arrived at by exposure to poetry and by his own experience in writing. He will have earned them in the process of growth and discovery.

10

As Poets Write

IT IS AN OPEN QUESTION how much is native to a child in his use of poetic devices and how much he has learned through exposure to poetry. We have already given some examples of the early use of imagery and we append here further ones by children of eight. Rachel writes:

> The sky is blue,
> The sun is yellow,
> And the grass blooms when the sun is yellow,
> And the flowers, too.
> Trees are *lighted up like Christmas trees,*
> They are so green.

Ellen writes:

THE SHADOW ON THE HILL

> When I look at the big red mountains,
> With the city below,
> I see the shadow of the city
> Lying on the mountains *like a sheet of grey paper*
> The shadows of the trees
> Are sometimes lying on it, too.

FAR-AWAY CLOUDS

> The far-away clouds
> Look just like the snow—
> A *mountain of snow,*
> A *mountain of marshmallows*
> Floating in the sky.

Sometimes when they are way up in the sky
They look *like cotton*—
All in little puffs.

A COLD WINTER EVENING

When a cold winter night comes,
The little snowflakes outside
Look *like spring blossoms*
Falling from their tree.

The sky *is their tree,*
And the *clouds are clusters*
Of more blossoms.

Again she writes, "The creek looks at me with its golden eyes," and
Karen, also eight, sees "the river in a golden dew."

When the children are older and have been reading poetry for some
time, they continue the use of imagery in their own writing, but how
deliberate this is it is impossible to determine. The same might be said,
however, of an adult poet. One can hardly imagine the latter saying
to himself, "I will put an image in here." The practice of poetry brings
with it a vocabulary of poetic usage, and the children draw upon this
as do their elders. Here follow examples of the use of imagery by older
children.

Rhoda, eleven, writes:

DREAMS

Dreams are queer—
Some are like walking in a labyrinth
Full of dusty cracks and holes,
With strange and weird creatures
Staring at you
From hidden places,
And an adventure
Ready to jump out and catch you,
When you are forced into a dark room
With cobwebs brushing and swinging past your face.
Then as you turn a corner,

A beautiful dream
Dressed in a starry gown,
With moons glittering in her hair,
And downy, golden wings
Flies away from you
To a place in the sky.

Rhoda was about to destroy this when I retrieved it and persuaded her
to keep it. The poem contains telling images: the labyrinth "full of dusty
cracks and holes," and the "dream dressed in a starry gown, with moons
glittering in her hair." In another poem she likens a leopard to "A
shadow that has no fear."

Bill, twelve, writes:

> Off in the distance there is a small lake,
> Set among the mountains like a glittering sapphire
> In a dull setting.
> It nestles there—mercury held in a cloth.

The last, "mercury held in a cloth," is an original concept and an apt
picture of a lake in the high altitudes.

Ross, eleven, likens the stars to "confetti some giant threw in the
sky," and Frank, eleven, likens darkness to "the last act in a play: The
scene changes, houses are changed into ghosts." (Curiously enough,
Frank now has taken up acting as his profession—one of two boys whose
early poems foreshadowed their later activities.)

Rose and Rena, twelve and thirteen respectively, avail themselves
of images. Rose:

GOLDFISH

Goldfish, I wonder how you feel in your house like a bubble.
Don't you ever get tired of going round and round,
Making the cat's eyes pop out,
Longing for just a bite of you?
The visitors admire your coat of golden sunset.
When I am lonely, I watch you open and close your mouth.
It makes me feel as if you were talking to me,
Then I no longer feel lonely.

Rena:

> The sky is like a huge ocean
> Which stretches forever,
> But unlike the sea,
> It is calm and serene,
> The clouds like small boats
> Floating on its waters.

Sean, twelve, writes:

NIGHT

> Night is still and dark and calm.
> The moon pours its silver generously
> Over the town.
> 'Most everyone sleeps at night
> In a calm and sleepful rest,
> Like an old flower
> Wilting its petals so quietly.

Sleep "like an old flower wilting its petals" is a beautiful and original image. In another image he likens the sea to a poem, "an endless poem which never stops."

Rae Jean, ten, in the first five lines of the following poem writes in true lyric cadence:

> It is late afternoon now.
> The shadows are long on the grass.
> The flowers gently wave to and fro
> And the birds rustle the leaves
> Under the oak trees as they walk.
> Now the sun is setting
> Behind the hills.
> Soon a swift breeze springs up.
> As the twilight deepens,
> The flowers turn into fairies,
> And dance in the light of the moon
> On into the night.
> Sometimes they sway and bend briskly

But now they are almost motionless,
Listening to the soft music
Played by the waving grasses.
Now the dawn breaks, and the gold of the morning
Washes over the fairies,
But look more closely,
They are not fairies at all,
But just flowers
Gleaming in the sunlight.

Except for the conventional intrusion of fairies, the poem contains fresh vision in the fairies bending "briskly," then being "almost motionless,/ Listening to the soft music/ Played by the waving grasses." And the "gold of the morning" is a charming designation of day.

The fact that the children know themselves to be engaged in writing poetry seems to impel them to avail themselves of the tools of poetry. The older they get the more they incorporate in their writing those devices that through their reading they have come to associate in their minds with poetry. As with their use of imagery, they employ certain devices unconsciously while they are still unaware of these as elements of poetry. John writes:

THE STEAM ENGINE

The steam engine starts with a snort,
The wheels creaking, the steam hissing,
The bell ringing, the fire-box glowing.
Faster, faster it goes,
Until it seems as if it is flying.
Through villages, through towns
It passes crossings with its whistle blowing.
Slower now, slower now.
Hiss goes the brake as it stops—
Its work is finished for the day.

Here we find the onomatopoetic words *snort, creaking, hiss* employed before the child had been introduced to them in a poetic context.

The children likewise employ inversion, the use of words out of their natural order. Katy, at eight, writes:

OUT BEYOND THE MOUNTAINS

Out beyond the mountains
There is a rushing river,
Trees at either end.
Tiny fish are living in the river,
Birds build their nests in the trees.
Bordering it are flowers.
Butterflies spread their golden wings
As they fly to the flowers for a rest.
There is grass all around the trees
Next to the flowers.
In the grass are little bugs,
They hop and chirp all day long.
They have a merry little song.
They sing, "This is a nice place to be."

In lines one, six, and eleven Katy makes use of inversion, thus giving a variety to the syntax.

Ross, at ten, writes: "A foggy day it is today," and, at eleven:

Softly, softly through the grass it moves,
Silently, peacefully and calm.
Paying no attention to people and their ways,
But snorts in disgust and moves on
Softly, silently and calm,
Paying no heed to wars, but goes on,
Without cheating or being cheated,
Softly, silently, peacefully and calm.

What it is that is moving through the grass, Ross does not tell us, but the mystery is reinforced by the inversion in the first line, repeated in the fifth and final ones. Joan, eleven, writes, "Out of the stillness comes a voice"; Herbert, "Only in the daytime the world is awake," and "Like ripples on the water,/ Blow the leaves forward and backward." Sometimes as in Katy's poem, the inversion may be used to break the monotony of subject and predicate order, sometimes to achieve a more cadential rendering as in the lines of Herbert. Needless to say, none of this is a conscious choice, but that makes it nonetheless valid and effective.

Personification, that device of speaking of inanimate objects as though they were persons, occurs in the younger as in the older children. Martha, at six, dictates:

> Candles, do you talk to somebody on the table
> When it's supper time?
> Red balloon, would you pop
> If I gave you a hit?
> Do you talk to anybody
> When you pop?
> You get a little hole in you
> When you pop, too.
> Do you know anybody who lives around the village
> When you go flying through the air
> And people try to catch you?
> What store did the people buy in
> That lost you, red balloon?

Rose, at eleven, writes:

> I have a plant of violets,
> And when I go to water them,
> They look at me with their yellow little eyes,
> They look so stern and serious,
> They make me take a step back,
> And say, "Oh!"

Joan, eleven, writes:

> "Day," said the sun, "we welcome you every morning
> With a friendly greeting.
> The flowers and trees bow and curtsy,
> The winds kiss you gently, and sometimes savagely,
> But always there is a welcome for you.
> Why do you not answer?
> Are you rude and have no manners?
> Please tell us why."
> The day did not answer,
> But smirked and walked on.

Emily, thirteen, writes:

DARKNESS

Night slowly takes day into its arms.
It also wishes to take me, I think—
The way it says,
"Please come and see me meet day."

As earlier mentioned, when the children employ rhyme they are driven into the most absurd ineptitudes. Too often the mere ability to concoct a set of rhyming lines is acclaimed by adults as something of a feat. Actually many children have great facility in spinning off rhymes, but the poems in which these occur are invariably trivial—a rehash of old ideas and subject matter generally unrelated to the child writing.

A few illustrations will suffice. An eight-year-old girl has an easy hand at rhyme, but note what she writes:

RAIN

The rain is good for the flowers,
    It makes them grow.
I like to stand in the rain
    And run about to and fro.
I like to hear the sound
    Of the pitter-patter on the ground.
Out of my window I always look
    To see if the water has made a brook.

While this contains no absurdities, it contains the trite phrases "to and fro" and "pitter-patter" and presents no fresh vision. Again she writes:

Little children playing in the night
    Are like little fireflies
With their sparkling lights.
    Playing on the side-walk,
    Playing in the street,
    But the nicest part
    Is when new neighbors meet.

Running, skipping, jumping,
   Playing to and fro,
Smelling pretty flowers,
   Playing in the snow.

Here we have the "to and fro" again and the incongruity of smelling pretty flowers in the snow. Both absurdity and/or incongruity are present in most of the younger children's rhymed poems, and the older ones are caught up in the same trap; there is no need for further illustrations. These examples indicate why I believe it is advisable to direct the children away from rhyming.

What they are able to write when they forego rhyme is evident in poems in which they tellingly express certain moods, as does Rachel in "Alone" quoted later, and Sean in "Night.'" Other instances of what children write when they are able to tap their own resources follow: Rhoda, eleven, writes:

There was no moon last night
As I walked into the garden.
In the silent darkness
Everything was different and queer.
The flowers were turned into goblins
Waiting to catch me.
I bumped into a tree whose long fingers grabbed,
And on whose branch was an owl—
Staring.
I ran away and saw a ghost
On Mother's clothes-line.
I went into the house
And turned on the lights.

Emily, thirteen, writes:

I am tired,
I walk slowly—
Everyone knows I am tired.

I am happy,
I walk fast,
Everyone knows I am happy.

Again she writes:

SLEEP

Sleep approaches me,
It lays warm soft hands on my eyes,
And makes the eyelids heavy.
First I am in a wakeful dream,
My eyes go blurry, I can't see straight.
My light I turn out,
And I lay my head on the soft smooth pillow.
Sleep's hands are stronger than my eyelids,
So I fall asleep.

This time I am in a true dream.
Nothing is blurry, but nothing is clear either.
Nothing stays in my mind.
I travel from one thought to another,
Yet each thought makes a firm impression on my mind.
Then I get terribly mixed up,
And I wake up.
I turn over and go to sleep,
And sleep quietly and soundly.

No one can question the authenticity of these experiences, and the dream sequence is one that everyone has shared; though not particularly poetically expressed, the poem is simple and genuine. Donna, too, writes of dreams:

I had a dream.
It was a wonderful dream of gladness.
I could hear it whisper
Soft words of joy in my ear.
It was like music coming in through my heart.
When I woke up I was sorry to leave it.

This, also, is authentic, but expressed with more poetic cadence than the previous poem.

Gary, eleven, writes:

PINE TREES

As a swift brisk wind sings through the tall stately pines,
A feeling of vastness comes over me . . .

Donna, twelve, writes:

Staring, staring at the endless sky
Makes you feel as though there were something else besides the blue—
That the universe could fit into.
But what would be beyond that?
When you think of it,
You have a feeling of emptiness and endlessness.

Kay, ten, writes:

LONELINESS

A still black shadow creeps over you at night
When you can't get to sleep—
　　Loneliness.

The same black shadow crawls over you again
When you are alone in the room—
　　Loneliness.

It happens to kings and queens,
It happens to beggar boys and beggar girls,
But it is always
　　Loneliness.

Even children as young as eight demonstrate at times a sense of form
by the use of repeated lines or refrains. Katy, at eight, writes:

The old wooden chest
Stands in the corner of the house
Waiting to be used some day.
It is a lonely sight
And full of cobwebs.
Nobody knows what's in it,
Because the key has been lost.

It stands there with nothing in, it,
Or maybe full of some treasure.
But nobody knows,
And will never find out
What is in the old wooden chest
Standing full of cobwebs
In the corner of the house.

By the same child:

THE PLANT BY THE WINDOW

The plant by the window
Is a green plant,
And has long leaves
Sprouting out of the roots.
To me it looks as though it was staring out
At the view below it.
The plant by the window
Sits in a tall white pot
On the window-sill.
It is staring out
At the view below it.

Such repetitions of lines are very common, even among older children who frequently frame their poems by repetition of the opening line at the end. Rachel, twelve, writes:

ALONE

Being alone is a queer feeling.
It brings you happiness and wonder.
You look for something
And never seem to find it.
You reach for that one thing.

I seem to realize things about our world—
New things—
I get the feeling of love, gentleness.
My feeling of being alone is a queer thing.

I find new impressions of people, places and things.
I get the feeling of someone creeping up behind me.
I turn quickly—no one's there.
I feel as though I'm trapped in a cage.

I enjoy being alone,
But also I get scared and frightened.
Being alone is a queer feeling.

This poem ranges somewhat wide, but the repetition of the opening phrase in line nine and again at the end serves to unify it.

Rena, at twelve, writes:

THE SKY

The sky is gray, just gray—
Only cloudy.
Only one black speck breaking through the gray.

It's a bird. It passes swiftly on its way.
Is it going home or just flying?
It's gone.

The sky is gray, just gray—
Only clouds again.

The repetition of the first line here seems to reinforce the poem's mood, as does the repetition in the poem "Loneliness" quoted earlier.

But the poem evincing the most intricate and elaborate sense of form is Kent's written at eleven:

OUR NAVY

A shadow passing before the sun
Signifies the passing of a dirigible,
    A torpedo on wings,
Guardian of the Navy's airplanes,
Spy on the enemy's movements.

A swish of water and a heavy swell,
Signifies the descending of a submarine,
    A great gray shark,
A destroyer of battleships,
Battleship of the depths of the sea.

A roar of motors, a heavy drone,
Like hundreds of bees from their hive,
    Swift little insects,
Fast messengers of the fleet,
Swift grey hornets with a deadly sting.

Like a piece of fog that has gone astray,
Its guns smoking and bellowing forth
A whale basking in the sun—
The Navy's floating fort.
Faithful fighter of the seas.

This poem, when analyzed, evinces not only an extraordinary organic form but great subtleties as well. Note, first, the poem is composed of four five-line stanzas, the third line of each being shorter than the others and presenting a metaphor of the particular craft described. Then each first line indicates the motion of the craft; each fourth and fifth lines, the function. In the first two stanzas the form of the second line is repeated, but obviating monotony, in the third stanza a metaphor is substituted for the previous "signifies." In the fourth stanza there is another modification—instead of the form of the opening lines of the other stanzas, this begins with a simile. And a certain climax is suggested by the order of presentation of the craft.

Of course all of this—structure and modifications—is (as is the case of all the children's employment of poetic devices) not done deliberately. But that makes the achievement nonetheless remarkable. Inspiration is impossible to analyze, and that such a poem as the above is not created in full consciousness of the artistic devices employed cannot be argued. Had such a poem been deliberately planned there is little doubt but that the result would have been different—the spontaneity would have been lost, and the organic unity might not have been present. We have noted previously what too great self-consciousness on the part of children leads to in their writing, but that a certain consciousness does arrive "after the fact" will be evident in the following chapter, in which will be treated the standards children have deduced from their reading and from the practice of writing.

11

Learning through Growth

THE CLASS is sitting around our large library table. We are ready to begin a poetry session. Before each child is his book in which he enters the poems chosen at our previous meeting, also the booklet containing poems of his own writing. One child asks, "Can't we read our own poems today instead of having our regular lesson?" I welcome the request since one of the reasons for making the booklets was precisely that of affording the children the opportunity for rereading their own poems. Also, the rereading may bring forth comments, which I surmise will have some significance. And the comments *are* forthcoming. I take these down, and date them, then later go to my files to ascertain the dates when the poems commented upon had been written. Given the date of the comment and the time lapse between it and the writing of the poem, I may be able to draw some conclusions as to what has happened to the child in the interval.

Let us note some of these poems and the comments on them. Katherine, ten, has written:

THE FIRE BELL

Whenever anybody pulls the long chain on the fire bell
It goes "Gong, Gong" as if to say, "Fire, Fire!"
Then the people run out of the building
To get the fire engines,
And pretty soon they come,
Ding, dong, cling, clang down the street.
Then the men put the fire out.
Then ding, dong, home they go.
"The fire is out," I say.

Reading this later, she says, "Cut out the 'I say.'" The deletion here is no doubt because of the irrelevance of the phrase, since there has been no previous use of "I" in the poem.

101

Joyce, ten, has written:

> The daffodils and the chrysanthemums
> Were standing straight one day,
> When there came a little wind
> That blew them all away.
> They blew and blew for miles and miles
> And then they landed on the ground.

She comments, "Tear it up. I don't like it." When a child gives no reason for changing or discarding a poem, one can only guess what the motivation is. In the present case, perhaps, though Joyce may not be conscious of the fact, she may feel that the poem is not related to experience; obviously it is not, since chrysanthemums and daffodils do not bloom at the same time of year. Note the use of rhyme in the second and fourth lines only—which will be discussed below.

Barbara, eleven, has written:

ACACIA SEASON

> Acacia has such pretty stems,
> And little yellow flowers,
> And when acacia's season's over,
> I wait and wait again.

She comments later, "I don't like the last line," which is again an irrelevant intrusion.

Emily, at eight, has dictated:

> Silvery moon so bright, so bright,
> Over the ocean,
> It is a full moon,
> But it does not give enough light
> For the ship to go.
> The ocean is silent
> And everybody is asleep.
> The rushing of the waves
> Makes the most noise.

On copying this poem for submission to the yearbook, Emily asked to omit line three, no doubt because of the prosy direct statement, but in any case the change is for the better.

Fay, nine, writes:

> Down by the ocean,
> Down by the bay,
> That's where I used to play.
> Sometimes with sand,
> Sometimes with rock,
> And then I'd go in wading,
> And it wouldn't be so cold—
> Down by the ocean,
> Down by the bay.

On reading this Fay strikes through the sixth and seventh lines. Again one can only guess the reason she does so, but here too we find a rhyme, once used then immediately abandoned. This is a characteristic procedure in the children's use of rhyme: they never feel a commitment to continuing with it.

These examples of deletions, chosen from among many, were made shortly after the poems had been written. Irrelevancy then seems to be one of the first criteria children bring to bear on their writing, and redundancy is a close second. But even young children, as does Katy, at eight, amend for aesthetic reasons:

> When winter comes
> The snow falls
> Right outside my house.
> It's soft, white and fluffy.
> It looks like powdered sugar.
> As I step into it I fall down.
>
> There are little prints in the snow
> Beside my own.
> They are the prints of the deer.
> From that I know
> They came to drink at night
> From the cool rushing stream.

At the session after writing this Katy amends the line, "As I step into it I fall down," to "As I step into it I sink down into the soft drifts," which is not only an improvement in cadence, but also gives a more sensory picture.

In the process of growing older the children discard their more childish concepts and expressions at the same time as they evaluate their writing by more mature aesthetic criteria. Likewise, since they have become more articulate and specific in their statements, they no longer oblige me to guess the reasons for changes or deletions.

Rachel, at twelve, writes:

TIMID SKY

Oh, huge sky, do you ever end?
You stretch your wings across the earth,
Your colors are so timid.
If you rain your tears,
The whole world is sad.
If you are filled with glory and sunshine,
The world is happy.
The food shelter people live on you.
Oh, blue sky, do you ever end
With your helping hand.

Reading this poem a year after writing it, Rachel says, "The line about food and shelter doesn't make sense." She deletes it and the final line. The metaphor of "raining your tears" is a telling one, also the sky stretching its "wings." Later she writes:

SHH!

How funny the street looks so bare,
The long paved road, the high buildings,
The tall telephone poles
Reaching high in front of each house.
But the house looks warm, still and welcoming.
I wonder what's inside that house.
I wonder if there is a blazing fire,
And some people talking softly around it.
But everything is so quiet.

Shh! I don't want to break my dream.
Then if I wake, I wake to reality:
A dirty street, tall ugly buildings,
A ragged house,

An unfriendly look upon its face,
An electric stove to heat the house,
And a hot sound of laughter.
How sad!

Shh! Don't wake me from my dream,
For it is hard to wake
And think of what you meant by this dream—
If it resembles anything specific.
Shh! Don't wake me.

Reading this a week after writing it, Rachel says, "It's terrible," but when I press her to define what is wrong,[1] she says, "Well, I don't always think this way." I reassure her: "One often has moods or feelings that are not habitual—it is quite all right to express them." Then she adds, "I don't like the line, 'If it resembles anything specific,' and the word *specific*." This is a sound criticism—the line and the word are prosy. From her criticism of the first poem on the score of sense, to that of the second on aesthetic grounds a year later, I feel we are justified in concluding that a certain growth has taken place. "A hot sound of laughter" is an original formulation.

Joan at thirteen writes:

> The boat was standing still
> When the dock began to slide backwards,
> Until it was left behind.[2]

Of this she says, "It's not a very good poem. It just makes a statement." Joyce makes a similar remark about her poem:

WAR

> Why should such a thing as war
> Be brought into a civilized country?
> If we were helpless and nothing else
> Could settle our arguments,

[1] Ordinarily I never press the children to define their objections, but in this case since Rachel tends to take refuge behind inarticulateness, I feel she may be helped by being induced to try to define her feelings.

[2] From Flora J. Arnstein, *Children Write Poetry* (New York: Dover Publications, Inc., 1967).

If we were savages and lived long ago,
I would not object—
But now what good does it do us,
Killing a thousand men,
Taking them from their families,
Killing a man you don't dislike.

Note that these children have discovered for themselves that mere statement of fact does not constitute poetry—that some transmutation has to occur in order that material may truly belong to the category of poetry. Also by the frequency of the remark "That sounds more like a story than a poem" the children are demonstrating their realization that uncadenced exposition is more in the province of prose than of poetry. At a very early age they sense the distinction, and the older children, although they may not make use of the word "story," often say, "It doesn't sound like a poem," as does one girl of her poem:

The little vine tries to climb up the wall,
Clinging to every little ledge that juts out,
Struggling to the top.
And when it gets to the top,
It climbs down the other side.

She is, of course, correct: there is nothing to distinguish this from straight prose.

David, twelve, writes:

THE DOOR

I know of a door, a singing door,
That sings the whole night through.
I know this door is fantasy,
Like a ghost or fairy tales,
Or a witch on a broom.
And when I go to sleep at night,
It sings and makes me fall asleep,
And then I dream of things I love,
That's why my door is so, so sweet.

Rereading this several months later, he says, "I don't like the last line," which obviously is out of key with the rest and also carries a sentimental aura which children almost invariably repudiate. He deletes this line and changes "I dream of things I love," to "I dream of what I love,"—which he may feel is more inclusive—extending *things* to *people*.

The consideration of certain words as being inappropriate to poetry—at least in certain contexts—dawns upon many children, as it did to Rachel with reference to the word *specific*. A girl of twelve has written:

LIFELESS

Fluffed is her hair in tight little curls,
Its softness has wandered far from life.
Her eyebrows are gone, a line takes their place,
Her lips are painted, unnatural they look,
Her cheeks are a soft fake pink.

Of this she says, "I don't like it," and a class member adds, "There shouldn't be *fake*. It's not a poetic word." The same girl writes:

Up the mountain by sunlight,
Trailing down in the pitch black night,
We waited for the moon.
But it came not that time.
So down the slopes we started,
Tumbling over one another,
Falling into hollows,
Till we reached our destination
Without the pale moon.

"I don't like it," she says, "especially the word 'destination'!"

Up to this point we have in the main been discussing the children's criticism of their own poems. We turn now to their comments on one another's. These comments rarely arose in the regular poetry sessions, but the following occurred when the children were engaged in selecting poems submitted for inclusion in their poetry yearbook. These "editorial" meetings brought forth a wealth of commentary, and it is from these occasions that most of the data relative to the development of criteria have been drawn.

The following poem was submitted by a twelve-year-old boy:

THOUGHTS

Looking across the mighty Pacific
With its vast waste of waters,
One thinks of Japan far off,
With its temples and palaces fair.
Then into your mind like a flash,
Comes the thought of the fighting between the
    Japanese and Chinese—
Their guns booming and flying like strong wind.
Suddenly your thoughts of far away
Cease with the loud noise of the surf.

One member of the editorial group comments (again): "It sounds like a story, not a poem"; another, "That line about the Japanese and Chinese is out of rhythm," noting even in the general nonrhythmic character of the poem the prosy awkwardness of the cadence.

A girl of twelve has submitted this poem:

FIRS

The firs hold their branches upward
Toward the sun and moon.
When the sun shines upon them.
The branches turn to a lighter, brilliant green,
And in the late afternoon
They give the rays of sunlight back to the sun,
And take on a new silver light from the moon.
In the morning they return the moonlight,
And receive the rays the sun has ready for them—
And this continues.

Hearing it read aloud she asks to withdraw it, without specific comment, but one member of the group says, "It sounds like a report." At another time the same girl is troubled about a poem she has written and asks for class comment.

From the light you cannot see to the dark
But from the dark you can see to the light.

If you have been in the light,
And try to find something in the dark,
You cannot find it.
But just the other way around,
If you have been in the dark,
You can find something in the light.[3]

"I don't like it," she says, "but I don't know why." "Well," says another girl, "it's just like *saying* things." Another comments, "It's too jerky." The writer then comes to her own evaluation: "I know. It's really not a poem at all."

Just as the children have arrived at a conception of the nature of poetry, so do they reach certain conclusions concerning infelicities, such as clichés, without ever having heard the concept formulated. Actually, in their own writing they make infrequent use of trite expressions. On one occasion a boy objects to a phrase descriptive of death: "No one can thwart its sting," by commenting, "It's not good—it's usual." One submission to the yearbook is the following:

This family is poor.
They have no fire in their fireplace
To give them cheery light.
They have no table in the room
On which to set their crusts of bread.
They have no bed
On which to rest their tired limbs.
This family is poor.

The above, by a boy of eleven, is scored by a girl: " 'Crusts of bread' and 'tired limbs' are too poetic," by which she undoubtedly means that they are clichés. Exception is taken to such poeticisms as "babe," and in one instance a girl discards her poem as being "too poemy," which probably means that she considers it spuriously poetic.

As with the case of clichés, so too the children without ever having heard of mixed metaphors criticize these as they appear in the following poem.

[3] The three poems above are from Arnstein, *Ibid.*

TWILIGHT

The twilight falls.
It cloaks the earth—
A grey and silent blanket,
And pushing through
Come tiny points of lights—
Showers of stars.[4]

One girl remarks: "The writer thought she ought to have images, but a *blanket* with *showers of stars!*"

Acclaim and appreciation of one another's poems are far more frequent than criticism. Of the poem "Our Navy" in the preceding chapter, one boy says, "It's a marvelous poem!" Another, "It has wonderful comparisons," which a girl amends with, "You mean images, don't you?" "I have only compliments for it," says another. Such commendations occur continuously—too many to quote.

Here, then, in this body of commentary by the children lies the answer to the question whether learning can take place without direct teaching. "How can the children learn if they are not told?" is the query frequently posed me. Can it be doubted that from the children's remarks we are being shown an emerging sense of what constitutes poetry, together with repudiation of prosy statement, clichés, inappropriate words, and, in cases of which I have not given illustrations, criticism of faulty rhythm? Surely this is evidence of growth. But such development does not take place in a vacuum. The children have derived their concepts through exposure to poetry, but mere exposure is not enough. Their attention has been constantly directed in the poems read them to the elements of poetry. Thus when they come to write their own poems, they unconsciously submit them to the concepts of poetry they have absorbed.

Still, it may be asked: Since the children are able to entertain such discrimination, why wait for them to arrive at it themselves? Why not tell them the good from the bad earlier? The question implies the fallacy of the assumption that telling presumes learning. Actually such telling frequently stands in the way of learning, for the' reason that criteria presented to the children often serve to confuse rather than to illumi-

---

[4] The two poems above are from *Ibid.*

nate. Not having reached the stage in their own development at which they are able to assimilate criteria (and no one can know just at what time they are able to do so), they are more likely than not to misapply them.

Let us suppose that the teacher has defined the word "prosy." It is in the nature of children to "latch onto" such a word because it carries with it an adult flavor, and then to apply it indiscriminately. But worse than this, they may be beset with the fear that what they write may be considered prosy, and in consequence they may suppress their spontaneous expression. Children are in such matters too prone to accept on authority. If the teacher designates something as good or bad they do not question; thus they are prevented from exercising their own judgment. And it is only by the exercise of judgment that they can arrive at valid evaluations—valid for them. By abdicating their genuine reactions they are losing touch with their inner source of aesthetic discrimination.

The acquiring of taste cannot be hurried; it can only be nourished and allowed to grow. It is, in any field, the product of exposure to works of superior quality over an expanse of time. Also by the wise and discriminating guidance of his teacher the young person is led through enjoyment and appreciation to the development of some measure of taste. The time element is important as well, for it takes time for certain values to become assimilated. One would not, for example, expect of a beginning student the response to poetic values that one would of a student who had been studying poetry for a year or so. Taste and discrimination are not matters of the mind alone. Poetry has its root not only in the intellect but in the emotions as well, and the young person in order to respond to it must have the experience of exploring (to a certain extent) his own emotions. He must, again through a period of time, have been in rapport with his own feelings in an atmosphere in which feelings are not only tolerated but valued. Taste requires time, guidance, and the proper environment in order to grow. Discrimination cannot be conferred by edict; it must be encouraged, and in order that such encouragement be not merely nominal the young people should even be permitted to express dislike of a poem the teacher may have brought to class. Nor should they be made to feel that this implies a criticism of him. They should have his sanction that there is room for preference in poetry as in everything else. Nor should the teacher insist that the children give reasons for their likes and dislikes. Formulation of values is too difficult (except as was the case with Rachel mentioned above). Our insistence upon formulation results frequently in rationalization, the children saying the first thing uppermost in their minds. By allowing a child to express his dislikes without censure, the teacher encourages in him the development of criteria which are available to him and valid for him at the given time.

This, then, is the case for growth. We adults too often err in not taking into account a child's potential; we need greater faith in him and in his inherent powers. In our eagerness to teach we sometimes encroach upon those areas of growth which offer the child the greatest opportunity for learning and the most lasting possibilities of enjoyment and appreciation.

12

To Speak for Oneself

THE TEACHER may at times be puzzled how to recognize authentic poetic expression in the children's poems. One of the earmarks is genuineness and a certain uniqueness: a child is speaking from himself, from his own feeling and observation. Of course this does not mean necessarily that the utterance is poetry, but at least it has that essential quality of poetry, the individual touch. As one boy put it, "Everyone writes about trees and rain and sky, but they should write about them differently." The difference lies in the fact that the writer has drawn upon his own experience, has not resorted to trite or derived expression, but has noted something distinctive, something to which he brings his own personal reaction. Joan, twelve, writes:

RUNNING RAIN

Watch the wind blowing the rain.
It looks as if each rain-drop
Is racing with the one ahead of it.
It seems to go straight across the sky.
It looks as if it's never falling,
Just racing on and on.

This, while not notably poetic, still draws upon individual observation, does not resort to the ready-made "pitter-patter" of rain.

Another mark of authenticity is unpretentiousness. When the children "go in for" *fancy* words, they are usually parroting something that they have read. Such parroting is especially evident when the children write in rhyme, as previously noted, and in their use of obsolete words and phrases. Often a truly felt experience seems to bring with it a poetic cadence, as is evident in the following two poems by Van, twelve:

113

A silence which is too quiet—
Then the rain.
It's raining—
With gusts of wind;

It's raining—
With sheets of water;
It's raining—
With dripping trees.

Then all is again still.
It has stopped.
A clearness settles—
Clear greens and blues,
And a dripping world
Is now outside.

The repetition of "It's raining" gives cadence to the poem while contributing to the sense of the continuing rain.

In the following poem the longer lines make for a quieter cadence, reinforced by the repetition of vowel sounds, the short "I" in *mist, dim,* and *thick* and the long "I" in *lightly, sky, whine, combines.*

The mist hangs lightly over the dim landscape,
The smoke blends with the soft sky.
Over where the mist is thick
The incessant whine of the fog horn
Combines with the early morning street sounds
Of the milkman's truck, and an occasional street car
To break noisily into the stillness.

Joyce, thirteen, writes:

I plunged into the silent pool—
The waters were silent and green,
And I pushed the water behind
Till I reached the other end.
Then I turned to look
At the silent green waters,

But the pool was in ripples—
My path could be seen,
And the silent green waters
Were no longer still.

The repetition of silent and green waters gives a cadential tone to the poem.

Donna writes:

THE END OF THE WORLD

The end of the world is far away.
It is way beyond the forest lake,
It is over a hundred oceans.
The birds will show you the way some time,
Perhaps today! Who knows?

. . . .

The shadows glare at me from the wall.
I look back at them thinking,
Why do you glare at me so?
But the shadows never answer.
They are quiet and black as a jungle.

Here in these two poems we have a child's own thoughts and imaginings not reminiscent of anything she may have read elsewhere.

A felt experience tends to bring with it a somewhat organic structure, so that the poem holds together with a sort of inherent logic. This is observable in many of the children's contemplative poems. Rena, thirteen, writes:

A tree strong and stalwart,
Leaning against a deep blue sky,
All alone in a sea of greenness. . . .

Play around me, Children!
Come to me, I'll give you shade
On a hot summer's day.

This falls naturally, though the child may not have written it in that way, into two clearly defined stanzas of three lines each.

Rachel, twelve, writes:

> Beauty is what?
> Is it the love for others,
> The tremendous rolling hills,
> The stars up above,
> The gentle faces,
> The wind-blown trees,
> The flowing stream?
>
> What is beauty?
> Did God create it,
> Or did it just come naturally?

Here structure may be said to reside in the unity of the poem—what has been said is complete, rounded off. The same is true of the following poem by the same girl:

> I took a trip to the sea shore.
> The wind was blowing harshly,
> And the waves were thumping,
> Pounding against the soft sandy earth's surface.
>
> The sky was so beautiful—
> The big shrilling streak of red and gray
> Mixed together so gracefully
> In front of the frosted blue sky.
>
> A cold spray from the ocean breeze
> Made me shiver from head to toe.
> I ran on the wet sand,
> The wind blowing my hair,
> I ran faster and faster,
> And jumped and fell into a sand pile,
> And rolled and rolled in the soft cool sand.
>
> I went back to the hot fire,
> And listened to the sounds of the beach—
> Ah, yes, all the sounds of the beach.

This is unmistakably authentic, rising into poetry in phrases such as "the frosted blue sky" and "the shrilling streak of red and gray."

David, aged twelve, writes the following:

THE OCEAN

The ocean is a funny thing.
The tide comes in, the tide goes out.
No one will ever know the deep mist mysteries
Of the white coral reef
That is beyond mankind's ideal.

The ocean is a mysterious thing,
Where its powerful hand
Hits its enemy, the land.
And at night time it goes to rest
And then starts a new mystery:
A mystery in death.

Here each stanza begins with a literal observation about the ocean but goes on to an imaginative and evocative conception that seems to have a symbolic connotation. This does not mean that the boy necessarily consciously recognizes any symbolic intent, but that there is often more involved in creative work than what is consciously planned is too evident to need argument.

Rachel writes:

DEATH

Death is the most frightening thing in the world to me.
You say to yourself that people manage to go on living,
But to me I feel as if the day will stop
When the people I love die.

I probably will go on living,
But to think that I'll never see them again!
I'm scared to think maybe some morning
I won't wake up to see the sun rise and fall,
Or to see my loved ones again.

To me it's hard to realize
How life is arranged in such a pattern.
Why does there have to be an end?

I never want to die or to leave the ones I love and hate.
I wonder why, Oh, why there is such a thing!
I'm very scared of death.

Here in this poem we have a child daring to plumb her thoughts and
feelings concerning the problem of life and death. It takes courage to
bring into words every man's deepest concern. But that the children have
this courage and that they grapple with thoughts that adults do not
usually credit them with having is abundantly proved by their poems.

Here are some poems in point. Carol at twelve writes:

> The wind is like a sudden thought:
> It blows wildly for a moment,
> Then settles down into itself
> And decides it is wrong.

Sean, twelve, writes:

DESIGN

> Design is a written form of man's wondering,
> Which leaves an abstract idea on the paper,
> But a real impression on a man's mind.

Design as a "written form of man's wondering" is surely an original
conception. Teachers will be astonished at the depth and range of
children's thinking, once the setting has been established in which the
children venture into their private world and have the courage to
reveal it.

Readers of this book may be inclined to think that too much space
has been accorded to the children's writing, but this has been done with
deliberate intent. In the writing is shown the children's own engagement with the aesthetic act, and it is through this engagement that they
seem to make the surest step in the direction of appreciation. By creative
writing they parallel the impulse that moves the adult poet to expression; they are introduced to the source of poetic utterance, which, in the
case any one child may not merit the term *inspiration*, but which at
least allows him a glimpse of what takes place in the mind of the poet.
And through his own effort he learns what goes into the making of

poetry—the cadence, the imagery, the "feeling-thought," and perhaps something of the proportion and balance that make of a poem a memorable utterance.

What children themselves think of poetry is best expressed in their own words. Sean asks:

> What is poetry?
> A written form of man's thoughts,
> Or a man's version of imagination?
> No one can really know except one . . .
> The poet.

Emily, ten, asks:

> What is poetry?
> Poetry is like the stars
> Left undiscovered . . .[1]

She touches here upon the limitless sweep of the poetic imagination. Donna, ten, gives her definition of poetry:

> Sunbeams are poems—
> All kinds of poems—
> They fill the air.
> Rain is poems, too—
> Diamond jets of poems.
> Fog is poems, too—
> Like a creeping tiger
> Ready to catch its prey.[2]

Donna realizes that poetry lies everywhere—"it fills the air," and she shares the poet's sensitive vision in her designation of rain as "diamond jets."

May we hope that by now this book has fulfilled its purpose: to demonstrate that poetry can be meaningful to children. By the references to poetry in the poems quoted above, and by the children's own poems, have they not shown that there exists a natural affinity between

---

[1] From Flora J. Arnstein, *Children Write Poetry* (New York: Dover Publications, Inc., 1967).
[2] From *Ibid.*

them and poetry? If this is true, then it remains for us teachers to provide the setting in which such an affinity may be discovered and enjoyed by the children. It rests with us to throw open the doors, to provide the welcome, and to play the gracious hosts, offering to share the bounty of poetry with our willing guests. Let us never be the ones to erect barriers to poetry enjoyment. Let us never be among those who strip children of their wings, who give justification for the sorry question posed by one frustrated child:

THE CANYON

Deep in the canyon all gray and green,
With a soft blue tint to the tops of the redwoods,
I would like so much to spread my wings,
And fly over you and listen to the roaring of the water.
　Who took away my wings?[3]

3 From *Ibid*.

ACKNOWLEDGMENTS

The author and publishers wish to thank the following publishers, authors, and agents for permission to reprint poems published in this book:

CURTIS BROWN, LTD. for "Jonathan Bing," by B. Curtis Brown. From *One Hundred Best Poems for Boys and Girls,* compiled by Marjorie Barrows. Whitman Publishing Co.

BURNS, OATES, AND WASHBOURNE, LTD. for "The Shepherdess," by Alice Meynell. From *The Poems of Alice Meynell.* Copyright ©, 1923, by Wilfred Meynell.

CONSTABLE AND COMPANY, LTD. for "Storm," by H. D. From *Sea Garden* by H. D. London: Constable and Co., Ltd., 1916.

NORMA MILLAY ELLIS for "Afternoon on a Hill" and "Travel," by Edna St. Vincent Millay. From *Collected Poems.* Harper & Row, Publishers. Copyright ©, 1917, 1921, 1945, 1948, by Edna St. Vincent Millay. By permission of Norma Millay Ellis.

HOLT, RINEHART AND WINSTON, INC. for "The Pasture" and "The Road Not Taken," by Robert Frost. *From Complete Poems of Robert Frost.* Copyright ©, 1916, 1921, 1930, 1939, by Holt, Rinehart and Winston, Inc. Copyright © renewed, 1944, by Robert Frost. Reprinted by permission of Holt, Rinehart and Winston, Inc. For the same poems, LAURENCE POLLINGER, LTD. From *Complete Poems of Robert Frost.* Published in the British Commonwealth by M/s Jonathan Cape, Ltd.

THE MACMILLAN COMPANY for "The Snare," by James Stephens. Reprinted with permission of the publisher from *Collected Poems,* by James Stephens. Copyright ©, 1915, by The Macmillan Company. Copyright ©, 1943, by James Stephens. And for "Full Moon," by Sara Teasdale. Reprinted with permission of the publisher from *Collected Poems,* by Sara Teasdale. Copyright ©, 1926 by The Macmillan Company; copyright ©, 1954, by Mamie T. Wheless.

A. D. PETERS for "Tarantella," by Hilaire Belloc, as Literary Agents for the Estate of Hilaire Belloc and his publisher, Gerald Duckworth and Company, Ltd.

THE SOCIETY OF AUTHORS for "The Listeners," by Walter de la Mare. Reprinted by permission of The Literary Trustees of Walter de la Mare and The Society of Authors as their representative.

STANFORD UNIVERSITY PRESS for poems quoted from *Adventure into Poetry,* by Flora Arnstein. Stanford University Press, 1951. Copyright ©, 1951, by the Board of Trustees of the Leland Stanford Junior University. All children's poetry in this book not reprinted from the volume above are manuscripts in the author's possession. (Reprinted by Dover Publications, Inc., 1967, as *Children Write Poetry: A Creative Approach.*)

THE VIKING PRESS, INC. for "The Noise of Waters," by James Joyce. From *Chamber Music,* copyright ©, by J. W. Heubsch; copyright ©, 1946, by Nora Joyce. In *Collected Poems,* Viking Press, Inc., 1937. Reprinted with permission of Viking Press, Inc.

INDEX OF FIRST LINES OF POETRY[1]

---

[1] For poems by children, the numeral after the name indicates the age of the child at the time the poem was written.

A CATALOGUE OF SELECTED DOVER BOOKS
IN ALL FIELDS OF INTEREST

A CATALOGUE OF SELECTED DOVER BOOKS IN ALL FIELDS OF INTEREST

AMERICA'S OLD MASTERS, James T. Flexner. Four men emerged unexpectedly from provincial 18th century America to leadership in European art: Benjamin West, J. S. Copley, C. R. Peale, Gilbert Stuart. Brilliant coverage of lives and contributions. Revised, 1967 edition. 69 plates. 365pp. of text.
21806-6 Paperbound $2.75

FIRST FLOWERS OF OUR WILDERNESS: AMERICAN PAINTING, THE COLONIAL PERIOD, James T. Flexner. Painters, and regional painting traditions from earliest Colonial times up to the emergence of Copley, West and Peale Sr., Foster, Gustavus Hesselius, Feke, John Smibert and many anonymous painters in the primitive manner. Engaging presentation, with 162 illustrations. xxii + 368pp.
22180-6 Paperbound $3.50

THE LIGHT OF DISTANT SKIES: AMERICAN PAINTING, 1760-1835, James T. Flexner. The great generation of early American painters goes to Europe to learn and to teach: West, Copley, Gilbert Stuart and others. Allston, Trumbull, Morse; also contemporary American painters—primitives, derivatives, academics—who remained in America. 102 illustrations. xiii + 306pp.
22179-2 Paperbound $3.00

A HISTORY OF THE RISE AND PROGRESS OF THE ARTS OF DESIGN IN THE UNITED STATES, William Dunlap. Much the richest mine of information on early American painters, sculptors, architects, engravers, miniaturists, etc. The only source of information for scores of artists, the major primary source for many others. Unabridged reprint of rare original 1834 edition, with new introduction by James T. Flexner, and 394 new illustrations. Edited by Rita Weiss. 6⅝ x 9⅝.
21695-0, 21696-9, 21697-7 Three volumes, Paperbound $13.50

EPOCHS OF CHINESE AND JAPANESE ART, Ernest F. Fenollosa. From primitive Chinese art to the 20th century, thorough history, explanation of every important art period and form, including Japanese woodcuts; main stress on China and Japan, but Tibet, Korea also included. Still unexcelled for its detailed, rich coverage of cultural background, aesthetic elements, diffusion studies, particularly of the historical period. 2nd, 1913 edition. 242 illustrations. lii + 439pp. of text.
20364-6, 20365-4 Two volumes, Paperbound $5.00

THE GENTLE ART OF MAKING ENEMIES, James A. M. Whistler. Greatest wit of his day deflates Oscar Wilde, Ruskin, Swinburne; strikes back at inane critics, exhibitions, art journalism; aesthetics of impressionist revolution in most striking form. Highly readable classic by great painter. Reproduction of edition designed by Whistler. Introduction by Alfred Werner. xxxvi + 334pp.
21875-9 Paperbound $2.25

VISUAL ILLUSIONS: THEIR CAUSES, CHARACTERISTICS, AND APPLICATIONS, Matthew Luckiesh. Thorough description and discussion of optical illusion, geometric and perspective, particularly; size and shape distortions, illusions of color, of motion; natural illusions; use of illusion in art and magic, industry, etc. Most useful today with op art, also for classical art. Scores of effects illustrated. Introduction by William H. Ittleson. 100 illustrations. xxi + 252pp.

21530-X Paperbound $1.50

A HANDBOOK OF ANATOMY FOR ART STUDENTS, Arthur Thomson. Thorough, virtually exhaustive coverage of skeletal structure, musculature, etc. Full text, supplemented by anatomical diagrams and drawings and by photographs of undraped figures. Unique in its comparison of male and female forms, pointing out differences of contour, texture, form. 211 figures, 40 drawings, 86 photographs. xx + 459pp. 5⅜ x 8⅜.

21163-0 Paperbound $3.00

150 MASTERPIECES OF DRAWING, Selected by Anthony Toney. Full page reproductions of drawings from the early 16th to the end of the 18th century, all beautifully reproduced: Rembrandt, Michelangelo, Dürer, Fragonard, Urs, Graf, Wouwerman, many others. First-rate browsing book, model book for artists. xviii + 150pp. 8⅜ x 11¼.

21032-4 Paperbound $2.00

THE LATER WORK OF AUBREY BEARDSLEY, Aubrey Beardsley. Exotic, erotic, ironic masterpieces in full maturity: Comedy Ballet, Venus and Tannhauser, Pierrot, Lysistrata, Rape of the Lock, Savoy material, Ali Baba, Volpone, etc. This material revolutionized the art world, and is still powerful, fresh, brilliant. With *The Early Work,* all Beardsley's finest work. 174 plates, 2 in color. xiv + 176pp. 8⅛ x 11.

21817-1 Paperbound $2.75

DRAWINGS OF REMBRANDT, Rembrandt van Rijn. Complete reproduction of fabulously rare edition by Lippmann and Hofstede de Groot, completely reedited, updated, improved by Prof. Seymour Slive, Fogg Museum. Portraits, Biblical sketches, landscapes, Oriental types, nudes, episodes from classical mythology—All Rembrandt's fertile genius. Also selection of drawings by his pupils and followers. "Stunning volumes," *Saturday Review.* 550 illustrations. lxxviii + 552pp. 9⅛ x 12¼.

21485-0, 21486-9 Two volumes, Paperbound $6.50

THE DISASTERS OF WAR, Francisco Goya. One of the masterpieces of Western civilization—83 etchings that record Goya's shattering, bitter reaction to the Napoleonic war that swept through Spain after the insurrection of 1808 and to war in general. Reprint of the first edition, with three additional plates from Boston's Museum of Fine Arts. All plates facsimile size. Introduction by Philip Hofer, Fogg Museum. v + 97pp. 9⅜ x 8¼.

21872-4 Paperbound $1.75

GRAPHIC WORKS OF ODILON REDON. Largest collection of Redon's graphic works ever assembled: 172 lithographs, 28 etchings and engravings, 9 drawings. These include some of his most famous works. All the plates from *Odilon Redon: oeuvre graphique complet,* plus additional plates. New introduction and caption translations by Alfred Werner. 209 illustrations. xxvii + 209pp. 9⅛ x 12¼.

21966-8 Paperbound $4.00

DESIGN BY ACCIDENT; A BOOK OF "ACCIDENTAL EFFECTS" FOR ARTISTS AND DESIGNERS, James F. O'Brien. Create your own unique, striking, imaginative effects by "controlled accident" interaction of materials: paints and lacquers, oil and water based paints, splatter, crackling materials, shatter, similar items. Everything you do will be different; first book on this limitless art, so useful to both fine artist and commercial artist. Full instructions. 192 plates showing "accidents," 8 in color. viii + 215pp. 8⅜ x 11¼.   21942-9 Paperbound $3.50

THE BOOK OF SIGNS, Rudolf Koch. Famed German type designer draws 493 beautiful symbols: religious, mystical, alchemical, imperial, property marks, lines, etc. Remarkable fusion of traditional and modern. Good for suggestions of timelessness, smartness, modernity. Text. vi + 104pp. 6⅛ x 9¼.
20162-7 Paperbound $1.25

HISTORY OF INDIAN AND INDONESIAN ART, Ananda K. Coomaraswamy. An unabridged republication of one of the finest books by a great scholar in Eastern art. Rich in descriptive material, history, social backgrounds; Sunga reliefs, Rajput paintings, Gupta temples, Burmese frescoes, textiles, jewelry, sculpture, etc. 400 photos. viii + 423pp. 6⅜ x 9¾.   21436-2 Paperbound $3.50

PRIMITIVE ART, Franz Boas. America's foremost anthropologist surveys textiles, ceramics, woodcarving, basketry, metalwork, etc.; patterns, technology, creation of symbols, style origins. All areas of world, but very full on Northwest Coast Indians. More than 350 illustrations of baskets, boxes, totem poles, weapons, etc. 378 pp.
20025-6 Paperbound $2.50

THE GENTLEMAN AND CABINET MAKER'S DIRECTOR, Thomas Chippendale. Full reprint (third edition, 1762) of most influential furniture book of all time, by master cabinetmaker. 200 plates, illustrating chairs, sofas, mirrors, tables, cabinets, plus 24 photographs of surviving pieces. Biographical introduction by N. Bienenstock. vi + 249pp. 9⅞ x 12¾.   21601-2 Paperbound $3.50

AMERICAN ANTIQUE FURNITURE, Edgar G. Miller, Jr. The basic coverage of all American furniture before 1840. Individual chapters cover type of furniture—clocks, tables, sideboards, etc.—chronologically, with inexhaustible wealth of data. More than 2100 photographs, all identified, commented on. Essential to all early American collectors. Introduction by H. E. Keyes. vi + 1106pp. 7⅞ x 10¾.
21599-7, 21600-4 Two volumes, Paperbound $7.50

PENNSYLVANIA DUTCH AMERICAN FOLK ART, Henry J. Kauffman. 279 photos, 28 drawings of tulipware, Fraktur script, painted tinware, toys, flowered furniture, quilts, samplers, hex signs, house interiors, etc. Full descriptive text. Excellent for tourist, rewarding for designer, collector. Map. 146pp. 7⅞ x 10¾.
21205-X Paperbound $2.00

EARLY NEW ENGLAND GRAVESTONE RUBBINGS, Edmund V. Gillon, Jr. 43 photographs, 226 carefully reproduced rubbings show heavily symbolic, sometimes macabre early gravestones, up to early 19th century. Remarkable early American primitive art, occasionally strikingly beautiful; always powerful. Text. xxvi + 207pp. 8⅜ x 11¼.   21380-3 Paperbound $3.00

ALPHABETS AND ORNAMENTS, Ernst Lehner. Well-known pictorial source for decorative alphabets, script examples, cartouches, frames, decorative title pages, calligraphic initials, borders, similar material. 14th to 19th century, mostly European. Useful in almost any graphic arts designing, varied styles. 750 illustrations. 256pp. 7 x 10. 21905-4 Paperbound $3.50

PAINTING: A CREATIVE APPROACH, Norman Colquhoun. For the beginner simple guide provides an instructive approach to painting: major stumbling blocks for beginner; overcoming them, technical points; paints and pigments; oil painting; watercolor and other media and color. New section on "plastic" paints. Glossary. Formerly *Paint Your Own Pictures*. 221pp. 22000-1 Paperbound $1.75

THE ENJOYMENT AND USE OF COLOR, Walter Sargent. Explanation of the relations between colors themselves and between colors in nature and art, including hundreds of little-known facts about color values, intensities, effects of high and low illumination, complementary colors. Many practical hints for painters, references to great masters. 7 color plates, 29 illustrations. x + 274pp. 20944-X Paperbound $2.50

THE NOTEBOOKS OF LEONARDO DA VINCI, compiled and edited by Jean Paul Richter. 1566 extracts from original manuscripts reveal the full range of Leonardo's versatile genius: all his writings on painting, sculpture, architecture, anatomy, astronomy, geography, topography, physiology, mining, music, etc., in both Italian and English, with 186 plates of manuscript pages and more than 500 additional drawings. Includes studies for the Last Supper, the lost Sforza monument, and other works. Total of xlvii + 866pp. 7⅞ x 10¾. 22572-0, 22573-9 Two volumes, Paperbound $10.00

MONTGOMERY WARD CATALOGUE OF 1895. Tea gowns, yards of flannel and pillow-case lace, stereoscopes, books of gospel hymns, the New Improved Singer Sewing Machine, side saddles, milk skimmers, straight-edged razors, high-button shoes, spittoons, and on and on . . . listing some 25,000 items, practically all illustrated. Essential to the shoppers of the 1890's, it is our truest record of the spirit of the period. Unaltered reprint of Issue No. 57, Spring and Summer 1895. Introduction by Boris Emmet. Innumerable illustrations. xiii + 624pp. 8½ x 11⅝. 22377-9 Paperbound $6.95

THE CRYSTAL PALACE EXHIBITION ILLUSTRATED CATALOGUE (LONDON, 1851). One of the wonders of the modern world—the Crystal Palace Exhibition in which all the nations of the civilized world exhibited their achievements in the arts and sciences—presented in an equally important illustrated catalogue. More than 1700 items pictured with accompanying text—ceramics, textiles, cast-iron work, carpets, pianos, sleds, razors, wall-papers, billiard tables, beehives, silverware and hundreds of other artifacts—represent the focal point of Victorian culture in the Western World. Probably the largest collection of Victorian decorative art ever assembled— indispensable for antiquarians and designers. Unabridged republication of the Art-Journal Catalogue of the Great Exhibition of 1851, with all terminal essays. New introduction by John Gloag, F.S.A. xxxiv + 426pp. 9 x 12. 22503-8 Paperbound $4.50

A HISTORY OF COSTUME, Carl Köhler. Definitive history, based on surviving pieces of clothing primarily, and paintings, statues, etc. secondarily. Highly readable text, supplemented by 594 illustrations of costumes of the ancient Mediterranean peoples, Greece and Rome, the Teutonic prehistoric period; costumes of the Middle Ages, Renaissance, Baroque, 18th and 19th centuries. Clear, measured patterns are provided for many clothing articles. Approach is practical throughout. Enlarged by Emma von Sichart. 464pp. 21030-8 Paperbound $3.00

ORIENTAL RUGS, ANTIQUE AND MODERN, Walter A. Hawley. A complete and authoritative treatise on the Oriental rug—where they are made, by whom and how, designs and symbols, characteristics in detail of the six major groups, how to distinguish them and how to buy them. Detailed technical data is provided on periods, weaves, warps, wefts, textures, sides, ends and knots, although no technical background is required for an understanding. 11 color plates, 80 halftones, 4 maps. vi + 320pp. $6\frac{1}{8}$ x $9\frac{1}{8}$. 22366-3 Paperbound $5.00

TEN BOOKS ON ARCHITECTURE, Vitruvius. By any standards the most important book on architecture ever written. Early Roman discussion of aesthetics of building, construction methods, orders, sites, and every other aspect of architecture has inspired, instructed architecture for about 2,000 years. Stands behind Palladio, Michelangelo, Bramante, Wren, countless others. Definitive Morris H. Morgan translation. 68 illustrations. xii + 331pp. 20645-9 Paperbound $2.50

THE FOUR BOOKS OF ARCHITECTURE, Andrea Palladio. Translated into every major Western European language in the two centuries following its publication in 1570, this has been one of the most influential books in the history of architecture. Complete reprint of the 1738 Isaac Ware edition. New introduction by Adolf Placzek, Columbia Univ. 216 plates. xxii + 110pp. of text. $9\frac{1}{2}$ x $12\frac{3}{4}$. 21308-0 Clothbound $10.00

STICKS AND STONES: A STUDY OF AMERICAN ARCHITECTURE AND CIVILIZATION, Lewis Mumford.One of the great classics of American cultural history. American architecture from the medieval-inspired earliest forms to the early 20th century; evolution of structure and style, and reciprocal influences on environment. 21 photographic illustrations. 238pp. 20202-X Paperbound $2.00

THE AMERICAN BUILDER'S COMPANION, Asher Benjamin. The most widely used early 19th century architectural style and source book, for colonial up into Greek Revival periods. Extensive development of geometry of carpentering, construction of sashes, frames, doors, stairs; plans and elevations of domestic and other buildings. Hundreds of thousands of houses were built according to this book, now invaluable to historians, architects, restorers, etc. 1827 edition. 59 plates. 114pp. $7\frac{7}{8}$ x $10\frac{3}{4}$. 22236-5 Paperbound $3.00

DUTCH HOUSES IN THE HUDSON VALLEY BEFORE 1776, Helen Wilkinson Reynolds. The standard survey of the Dutch colonial house and outbuildings, with constructional features, decoration, and local history associated with individual homesteads. Introduction by Franklin D. Roosevelt. Map. 150 illustrations. 469pp. $6\frac{5}{8}$ x $9\frac{1}{4}$. 21469-9 Paperbound $3.50

AGAINST THE GRAIN (A REBOURS), Joris K. Huysmans. Filled with weird images, evidences of a bizarre imagination, exotic experiments with hallucinatory drugs, rich tastes and smells and the diversions of its sybarite hero Duc Jean des Esseintes, this classic novel pushed 19th-century literary decadence to its limits. Full unabridged edition. Do not confuse this with abridged editions generally sold. Introduction by Havelock Ellis. xlix + 206pp. 22190-3 Paperbound $2.00

VARIORUM SHAKESPEARE: HAMLET. Edited by Horace H. Furness; a landmark of American scholarship. Exhaustive footnotes and appendices treat all doubtful words and phrases, as well as suggested critical emendations throughout the play's history. First volume contains editor's own text, collated with all Quartos and Folios. Second volume contains full first Quarto, translations of Shakespeare's sources (Belleforest, and Saxo Grammaticus), Der Bestrafte Brudermord, and many essays on critical and historical points of interest by major authorities of past and present. Includes details of staging and costuming over the years. By far the best edition available for serious students of Shakespeare. Total of xx + 905pp.
21004-9, 21005-7, 2 volumes, Paperbound $5.25

A LIFE OF WILLIAM SHAKESPEARE, Sir Sidney Lee. This is the standard life of Shakespeare, summarizing everything known about Shakespeare and his plays. Incredibly rich in material, broad in coverage, clear and judicious, it has served thousands as the best introduction to Shakespeare. 1931 edition. 9 plates. xxix + 792pp. (USO) 21967-4 Paperbound $3.75

MASTERS OF THE DRAMA, John Gassner. Most comprehensive history of the drama in print, covering every tradition from Greeks to modern Europe and America, including India, Far East, etc. Covers more than 800 dramatists, 2000 plays, with biographical material, plot summaries, theatre history, criticism, etc. "Best of its kind in English," New Republic. 77 illustrations. xxii + 890pp.
20100-7 Clothbound $7.50

THE EVOLUTION OF THE ENGLISH LANGUAGE, George McKnight. The growth of English, from the 14th century to the present. Unusual, non-technical account presents basic information in very interesting form: sound shifts, change in grammar and syntax, vocabulary growth, similar topics. Abundantly illustrated with quotations. Formerly Modern English in the Making. xii + 590pp.
21932-1 Paperbound $3.50

AN ETYMOLOGICAL DICTIONARY OF MODERN ENGLISH, Ernest Weekley. Fullest, richest work of its sort, by foremost British lexicographer. Detailed word histories, including many colloquial and archaic words; extensive quotations. Do not confuse this with the Concise Etymological Dictionary, which is much abridged. Total of xxvii + 830pp. 6½ x 9¼.
21873-2, 21874-0 Two volumes, Paperbound $5.50

FLATLAND: A ROMANCE OF MANY DIMENSIONS, E. A. Abbott. Classic of science-fiction explores ramifications of life in a two-dimensional world, and what happens when a three-dimensional being intrudes. Amusing reading, but also useful as introduction to thought about hyperspace. Introduction by Banesh Hoffmann. 16 illustrations. xx + 103pp. 20001-9 Paperbound $1.00

POEMS OF ANNE BRADSTREET, edited with an introduction by Robert Hutchinson. A new selection of poems by America's first poet and perhaps the first significant woman poet in the English language. 48 poems display her development in works of considerable variety—love poems, domestic poems, religious meditations, formal elegies, "quaternions," etc. Notes, bibliography. viii + 222pp.

22160-1 Paperbound $2.00

THREE GOTHIC NOVELS: THE CASTLE OF OTRANTO BY HORACE WALPOLE; VATHEK BY WILLIAM BECKFORD; THE VAMPYRE BY JOHN POLIDORI, WITH FRAGMENT OF A NOVEL BY LORD BYRON, edited by E. F. Bleiler. The first Gothic novel, by Walpole; the finest Oriental tale in English, by Beckford; powerful Romantic supernatural story in versions by Polidori and Byron. All extremely important in history of literature; all still exciting, packed with supernatural thrills, ghosts, haunted castles, magic, etc. xl + 291pp.

21232-7 Paperbound $2.00

THE BEST TALES OF HOFFMANN, E. T. A. Hoffmann. 10 of Hoffmann's most important stories, in modern re-editings of standard translations: Nutcracker and the King of Mice, Signor Formica, Automata, The Sandman, Rath Krespel, The Golden Flowerpot, Master Martin the Cooper, The Mines of Falun, The King's Betrothed, A New Year's Eve Adventure. 7 illustrations by Hoffmann. Edited by E. F. Bleiler. xxxix + 419pp.

21793-0 Paperbound $2.25

GHOST AND HORROR STORIES OF AMBROSE BIERCE, Ambrose Bierce. 23 strikingly modern stories of the horrors latent in the human mind: The Eyes of the Panther, The Damned Thing, An Occurrence at Owl Creek Bridge, An Inhabitant of Carcosa, etc., plus the dream-essay, Visions of the Night. Edited by E. F. Bleiler. xxii + 199pp.

20767-6 Paperbound $1.50

BEST GHOST STORIES OF J. S. LeFANU, J. Sheridan LeFanu. Finest stories by Victorian master often considered greatest supernatural writer of all. Carmilla, Green Tea, The Haunted Baronet, The Familiar, and 12 others. Most never before available in the U. S. A. Edited by E. F. Bleiler. 8 illustrations from Victorian publications. xvii + 467pp.

20415-4 Paperbound $2.50

THE TIME STREAM, THE GREATEST ADVENTURE, AND THE PURPLE SAPPHIRE—THREE SCIENCE FICTION NOVELS, John Taine (Eric Temple Bell). Great American mathematician was also foremost science fiction novelist of the 1920's. *The Time Stream,* one of all-time classics, uses concepts of circular time; *The Greatest Adventure,* incredibly ancient biological experiments from Antarctica threaten to escape; The *Purple Sapphire,* superscience, lost races in Central Tibet, survivors of the Great Race. 4 illustrations by Frank R. Paul. v + 532pp.

21180-0 Paperbound $2.50

SEVEN SCIENCE FICTION NOVELS, H. G. Wells. The standard collection of the great novels. Complete, unabridged. *First Men in the Moon, Island of Dr. Moreau, War of the Worlds, Food of the Gods, Invisible Man, Time Machine, In the Days of the Comet.* Not only science fiction fans, but every educated person owes it to himself to read these novels. 1015pp.

20264-X Clothbound $5.00

INCIDENTS OF TRAVEL IN YUCATAN, John L. Stephens. Classic (1843) exploration of jungles of Yucatan, looking for evidences of Maya civilization. Stephens found many ruins; comments on travel adventures, Mexican and Indian culture. 127 striking illustrations by F. Catherwood. Total of 669 pp.

20926-1, 20927-X Two volumes, Paperbound $5.00

INCIDENTS OF TRAVEL IN CENTRAL AMERICA, CHIAPAS, AND YUCATAN, John L. Stephens. An exciting travel journal and an important classic of archeology. Narrative relates his almost single-handed discovery of the Mayan culture, and exploration of the ruined cities of Copan, Palenque, Utatlan and others; the monuments they dug from the earth, the temples buried in the jungle, the customs of poverty-stricken Indians living a stone's throw from the ruined palaces. 115 drawings by F. Catherwood. Portrait of Stephens. xii + 812pp.

22404-X, 22405-8 Two volumes, Paperbound $6.00

A NEW VOYAGE ROUND THE WORLD, William Dampier. Late 17-century naturalist joined the pirates of the Spanish Main to gather information; remarkably vivid account of buccaneers, pirates; detailed, accurate account of botany, zoology, ethnography of lands visited. Probably the most important early English voyage, enormous implications for British exploration, trade, colonial policy. Also most interesting reading. Argonaut edition, introduction by Sir Albert Gray. New introduction by Percy Adams. 6 plates, 7 illustrations. xlvii + 376pp. 6½ x 9¼.

21900-3 Paperbound $3.00

INTERNATIONAL AIRLINE PHRASE BOOK IN SIX LANGUAGES, Joseph W. Bátor. Important phrases and sentences in English paralleled with French, German, Portuguese, Italian, Spanish equivalents, covering all possible airport-travel situations; created for airline personnel as well as tourist by Language Chief, Pan American Airlines. xiv + 204pp.

22017-6 Paperbound $2.00

STAGE COACH AND TAVERN DAYS, Alice Morse Earle. Detailed, lively account of the early days of taverns; their uses and importance in the social, political and military life; furnishings and decorations; locations; food and drink; tavern signs, etc. Second half covers every aspect of early travel; the roads, coaches, drivers, etc. Nostalgic, charming, packed with fascinating material. 157 illustrations, mostly photographs. xiv + 449pp.

22518-6 Paperbound $4.00

NORSE DISCOVERIES AND EXPLORATIONS IN NORTH AMERICA, Hjalmar R. Holand. The perplexing Kensington Stone, found in Minnesota at the end of the 19th century. Is it a record of a Scandinavian expedition to North America in the 14th century? Or is it one of the most successful hoaxes in history. A scientific detective investigation. Formerly *Westward from Vinland*. 31 photographs, 17 figures. x + 354pp.

22014-1 Paperbound $2.75

A BOOK OF OLD MAPS, compiled and edited by Emerson D. Fite and Archibald Freeman. 74 old maps offer an unusual survey of the discovery, settlement and growth of America down to the close of the Revolutionary war: maps showing Norse settlements in Greenland, the explorations of Columbus, Verrazano, Cabot, Champlain, Joliet, Drake, Hudson, etc., campaigns of Revolutionary war battles, and much more. Each map is accompanied by a brief historical essay. xvi + 299pp. 11 x 13¾.

22084-2 Paperbound $6.00

THE RED FAIRY BOOK, Andrew Lang. Lang's color fairy books have long been children's favorites. This volume includes Rapunzel, Jack and the Bean-stalk and 35 other stories, familiar and unfamiliar. 4 plates, 93 illustrations x + 367pp.

21673-X Paperbound $1.95

THE BLUE FAIRY BOOK, Andrew Lang. Lang's tales come from all countries and all times. Here are 37 tales from Grimm, the Arabian Nights, Greek Mythology, and other fascinating sources. 8 plates, 130 illustrations. xi + 390pp.

21437-0 Paperbound $1.95

HOUSEHOLD STORIES BY THE BROTHERS GRIMM. Classic English-language edition of the well-known tales — Rumpelstiltskin, Snow White, Hansel and Gretel, The Twelve Brothers, Faithful John, Rapunzel, Tom Thumb (52 stories in all). Translated into simple, straightforward English by Lucy Crane. Ornamented with headpieces, vignettes, elaborate decorative initials and a dozen full-page illustrations by Walter Crane. x + 269pp. 21080-4 Paperbound $1.75

THE MERRY ADVENTURES OF ROBIN HOOD, Howard Pyle. The finest modern versions of the traditional ballads and tales about the great English outlaw. Howard Pyle's complete prose version, with every word, every illustration of the first edition. Do not confuse this facsimile of the original (1883) with modern editions that change text or illustrations. 23 plates plus many page decorations. xxii + 296pp.

22043-5 Paperbound $2.00

THE STORY OF KING ARTHUR AND HIS KNIGHTS, Howard Pyle. The finest children's version of the life of King Arthur; brilliantly retold by Pyle, with 48 of his most imaginative illustrations. xviii + 313pp. 6⅛ x 9¼.

21445-1 Paperbound $2.00

THE WONDERFUL WIZARD OF OZ, L. Frank Baum. America's finest children's book in facsimile of first edition with all Denslow illustrations in full color. The edition a child should have. Introduction by Martin Gardner. 23 color plates, scores of drawings. iv + 267pp. 20691-2 Paperbound $1.95

THE MARVELOUS LAND OF OZ, L. Frank Baum. The second Oz book, every bit as imaginative as the Wizard. The hero is a boy named Tip, but the Scarecrow and the Tin Woodman are back, as is the Oz magic. 16 color plates, 120 drawings by John R. Neill. 287pp. 20692-0 Paperbound $1.75

THE MAGICAL MONARCH OF MO, L. Frank Baum. Remarkable adventures in a land even stranger than Oz. The best of Baum's books not in the Oz series. 15 color plates and dozens of drawings by Frank Verbeck. xviii + 237pp.

21892-9 Paperbound $2.00

THE BAD CHILD'S BOOK OF BEASTS, MORE BEASTS FOR WORSE CHILDREN, A MORAL ALPHABET, Hilaire Belloc. Three complete humor classics in one volume. Be kind to the frog, and do not call him names . . . and 28 other whimsical animals. Familiar favorites and some not so well known. Illustrated by Basil Blackwell. 156pp. (USO) 20749-8 Paperbound $1.25

EAST O' THE SUN AND WEST O' THE MOON, George W. Dasent. Considered the best of all translations of these Norwegian folk tales, this collection has been enjoyed by generations of children (and folklorists too). Includes True and Untrue, Why the Sea is Salt, East O' the Sun and West O' the Moon, Why the Bear is Stumpy-Tailed, Boots and the Troll, The Cock and the Hen, Rich Peter the Pedlar, and 52 more. The only edition with all 59 tales. 77 illustrations by Erik Werenskiold and Theodor Kittelsen. xv + 418pp.   22521-6 Paperbound $3.00

GOOPS AND HOW TO BE THEM, Gelett Burgess. Classic of tongue-in-cheek humor, masquerading as etiquette book. 87 verses, twice as many cartoons, show mischievous Goops as they demonstrate to children virtues of table manners, neatness, courtesy, etc. Favorite for generations. viii + 88pp. 6½ x 9¼.
                                                            22233-0 Paperbound $1.25

ALICE'S ADVENTURES UNDER GROUND, Lewis Carroll. The first version, quite different from the final Alice in Wonderland, printed out by Carroll himself with his own illustrations. Complete facsimile of the "million dollar" manuscript Carroll gave to Alice Liddell in 1864. Introduction by Martin Gardner. viii + 96pp. Title and dedication pages in color.   21482-6 Paperbound $1.00

THE BROWNIES, THEIR BOOK, Palmer Cox. Small as mice, cunning as foxes, exuberant and full of mischief, the Brownies go to the zoo, toy shop, seashore, circus, etc., in 24 verse adventures and 266 illustrations. Long a favorite, since their first appearance in St. Nicholas Magazine. xi + 144pp. 6⅝ x 9¼.
                                                            21265-3 Paperbound $1.50

SONGS OF CHILDHOOD, Walter De La Mare. Published (under the pseudonym Walter Ramal) when De La Mare was only 29, this charming collection has long been a favorite children's book. A facsimile of the first edition in paper, the 47 poems capture the simplicity of the nursery rhyme and the ballad, including such lyrics as I Met Eve, Tartary, The Silver Penny. vii + 106pp. 21972-0 Paperbound $1.25

THE COMPLETE NONSENSE OF EDWARD LEAR, Edward Lear. The finest 19th-century humorist-cartoonist in full: all nonsense limericks, zany alphabets, Owl and Pussycat, songs, nonsense botany, and more than 500 illustrations by Lear himself. Edited by Holbrook Jackson. xxix + 287pp.   (USO) 20167-8 Paperbound $1.75

BILLY WHISKERS: THE AUTOBIOGRAPHY OF A GOAT, Frances Trego Montgomery. A favorite of children since the early 20th century, here are the escapades of that rambunctious, irresistible and mischievous goat—Billy Whiskers. Much in the spirit of Peck's Bad Boy, this is a book that children never tire of reading or hearing. All the original familiar illustrations by W. H. Fry are included: 6 color plates, 18 black and white drawings. 159pp.   22345-0 Paperbound $2.00

MOTHER GOOSE MELODIES. Faithful republication of the fabulously rare Munroe and Francis "copyright 1833" Boston edition—the most important Mother Goose collection, usually referred to as the "original." Familiar rhymes plus many rare ones, with wonderful old woodcut illustrations. Edited by E. F. Bleiler. 128pp. 4½ x 6⅜.   22577-1 Paperbound $1.25

TWO LITTLE SAVAGES; BEING THE ADVENTURES OF TWO BOYS WHO LIVED AS INDIANS AND WHAT THEY LEARNED, Ernest Thompson Seton. Great classic of nature and boyhood provides a vast range of woodlore in most palatable form, a genuinely entertaining story. Two farm boys build a teepee in woods and live in it for a month, working out Indian solutions to living problems, star lore, birds and animals, plants, etc. 293 illustrations. vii + 286pp.

20985-7 Paperbound $1.95

PETER PIPER'S PRACTICAL PRINCIPLES OF PLAIN & PERFECT PRONUNCIATION. Alliterative jingles and tongue-twisters of surprising charm, that made their first appearance in America about 1830. Republished in full with the spirited woodcut illustrations from this earliest American edition. 32pp. $4\frac{1}{2}$ x $6\frac{3}{8}$.

22560-7 Paperbound $1.00

SCIENCE EXPERIMENTS AND AMUSEMENTS FOR CHILDREN, Charles Vivian. 73 easy experiments, requiring only materials found at home or easily available, such as candles, coins, steel wool, etc.; illustrate basic phenomena like vacuum, simple chemical reaction, etc. All safe. Modern, well-planned. Formerly *Science Games for Children*. 102 photos, numerous drawings. 96pp. $6\frac{1}{8}$ x $9\frac{1}{4}$.

21856-2 Paperbound $1.25

AN INTRODUCTION TO CHESS MOVES AND TACTICS SIMPLY EXPLAINED, Leonard Barden. Informal intermediate introduction, quite strong in explaining reasons for moves. Covers basic material, tactics, important openings, traps, positional play in middle game, end game. Attempts to isolate patterns and recurrent configurations. Formerly *Chess*. 58 figures. 102pp. (USO) 21210-6 Paperbound $1.25

LASKER'S MANUAL OF CHESS, Dr. Emanuel Lasker. Lasker was not only one of the five great World Champions, he was also one of the ablest expositors, theorists, and analysts. In many ways, his Manual, permeated with his philosophy of battle, filled with keen insights, is one of the greatest works ever written on chess. Filled with analyzed games by the great players. A single-volume library that will profit almost any chess player, beginner or master. 308 diagrams. xli x 349pp.

20640-8 Paperbound $2.50

THE MASTER BOOK OF MATHEMATICAL RECREATIONS, Fred Schuh. In opinion of many the finest work ever prepared on mathematical puzzles, stunts, recreations; exhaustively thorough explanations of mathematics involved, analysis of effects, citation of puzzles and games. Mathematics involved is elementary. Translated by F. Göbel. 194 figures. xxiv + 430pp.

22134-2 Paperbound $3.00

MATHEMATICS, MAGIC AND MYSTERY, Martin Gardner. Puzzle editor for Scientific American explains mathematics behind various mystifying tricks: card tricks, stage "mind reading," coin and match tricks, counting out games, geometric dissections, etc. Probability sets, theory of numbers clearly explained. Also provides more than 400 tricks, guaranteed to work, that you can do. 135 illustrations. xii + 176pp.

20338-2 Paperbound $1.50

"ESSENTIAL GRAMMAR" SERIES

All you really need to know about modern, colloquial grammar. Many educational shortcuts help you learn faster, understand better. Detailed cognate lists teach you to recognize similarities between English and foreign words and roots—make learning vocabulary easy and interesting. Excellent for independent study or as a supplement to record courses.

ESSENTIAL FRENCH GRAMMAR, Seymour Resnick. 2500-item cognate list. 159pp.
(EBE) 20419-7 Paperbound $1.25

ESSENTIAL GERMAN GRAMMAR, Guy Stern and Everett F. Bleiler. Unusual shortcuts on noun declension, word order, compound verbs. 124pp.
(EBE) 20422-7 Paperbound $1.25

ESSENTIAL ITALIAN GRAMMAR, Olga Ragusa. 111pp.
(EBE) 20779-X Paperbound $1.25

ESSENTIAL JAPANESE GRAMMAR, Everett F. Bleiler. In Romaji transcription; no characters needed. Japanese grammar is regular and simple. 156pp.
21027-8 Paperbound $1.25

ESSENTIAL PORTUGUESE GRAMMAR, Alexander da R. Prista. vi + 114pp.
21650-0 Paperbound $1.25

ESSENTIAL SPANISH GRAMMAR, Seymour Resnick. 2500 word cognate list. 115pp.
(EBE) 20780-3 Paperbound $1.25

ESSENTIAL ENGLISH GRAMMAR, Philip Gucker. Combines best features of modern, functional and traditional approaches. For refresher, class use, home study. x + 177pp.
21649-7 Paperbound $1.25

A PHRASE AND SENTENCE DICTIONARY OF SPOKEN SPANISH. Prepared for U. S. War Department by U. S. linguists. As above, unit is idiom, phrase or sentence rather than word. English-Spanish and Spanish-English sections contain modern equivalents of over 18,000 sentences. Introduction and appendix as above. iv + 513pp.
20495-2 Paperbound $2.00

A PHRASE AND SENTENCE DICTIONARY OF SPOKEN RUSSIAN. Dictionary prepared for U. S. War Department by U. S. linguists. Basic unit is not the word, but the idiom, phrase or sentence. English-Russian and Russian-English sections contain modern equivalents for over 30,000 phrases. Grammatical introduction covers phonetics, writing, syntax. Appendix of word lists for food, numbers, geographical names, etc. vi + 573 pp. 6⅛ x 9¼.
20496-0 Paperbound $3.00

CONVERSATIONAL CHINESE FOR BEGINNERS, Morris Swadesh. Phonetic system, beginner's course in Pai Hua Mandarin Chinese covering most important, most useful speech patterns. Emphasis on modern colloquial usage. Formerly *Chinese in Your Pocket.* xvi + 158pp.
21123-1 Paperbound $1.50

How to Know the Wild Flowers, Mrs. William Starr Dana. This is the classical book of American wildflowers (of the Eastern and Central United States), used by hundreds of thousands. Covers over 500 species, arranged in extremely easy to use color and season groups. Full descriptions, much plant lore. This Dover edition is the fullest ever compiled, with tables of nomenclature changes. 174 full-page plates by M. Satterlee. xii + 418pp.　　　20332-8 Paperbound $2.50

Our Plant Friends and Foes, William Atherton DuPuy. History, economic importance, essential botanical information and peculiarities of 25 common forms of plant life are provided in this book in an entertaining and charming style. Covers food plants (potatoes, apples, beans, wheat, almonds, bananas, etc.), flowers (lily, tulip, etc.), trees (pine, oak, elm, etc.), weeds, poisonous mushrooms and vines, gourds, citrus fruits, cotton, the cactus family, and much more. 108 illustrations. xiv + 290pp.　　　22272-1 Paperbound $2.00

How to Know the Ferns, Frances T. Parsons. Classic survey of Eastern and Central ferns, arranged according to clear, simple identification key. Excellent introduction to greatly neglected nature area. 57 illustrations and 42 plates. xvi + 215pp.　　　20740-4 Paperbound $1.75

Manual of the Trees of North America, Charles S. Sargent. America's foremost dendrologist provides the definitive coverage of North American trees and tree-like shrubs. 717 species fully described and illustrated: exact distribution, down to township; full botanical description; economic importance; description of subspecies and races; habitat, growth data; similar material. Necessary to every serious student of tree-life. Nomenclature revised to present. Over 100 locating keys. 783 illustrations. lii + 934pp. 20277-1, 20278-X Two volumes, Paperbound $6.00

Our Northern Shrubs, Harriet L. Keeler. Fine non-technical reference work identifying more than 225 important shrubs of Eastern and Central United States and Canada. Full text covering botanical description, habitat, plant lore, is paralleled with 205 full-page photographs of flowering or fruiting plants. Nomenclature revised by Edward G. Voss. One of few works concerned with shrubs. 205 plates, 35 drawings. xxviii + 521pp.　　　21989-5 Paperbound $3.75

The Mushroom Handbook, Louis C. C. Krieger. Still the best popular handbook: full descriptions of 259 species, cross references to another 200. Extremely thorough text enables you to identify, know all about any mushroom you are likely to meet in eastern and central U. S. A.: habitat, luminescence, poisonous qualities, use, folklore, etc. 32 color plates show over 50 mushrooms, also 126 other illustrations. Finding keys. vii + 560pp.　　　21861-9 Paperbound $3.95

Handbook of Birds of Eastern North America, Frank M. Chapman. Still much the best single-volume guide to the birds of Eastern and Central United States. Very full coverage of 675 species, with descriptions, life habits, distribution, similar data. All descriptions keyed to two-page color chart. With this single volume the average birdwatcher needs no other books. 1931 revised edition. 195 illustrations. xxxvi + 581pp.　　　21489-3 Paperbound $3.25

MATHEMATICAL PUZZLES FOR BEGINNERS AND ENTHUSIASTS, Geoffrey Mott-Smith. 189 puzzles from easy to difficult—involving arithmetic, logic, algebra, properties of digits, probability, etc.—for enjoyment and mental stimulus. Explanation of mathematical principles behind the puzzles. 135 illustrations. viii + 248pp.
20198-8 Paperbound $1.25

PAPER FOLDING FOR BEGINNERS, William D. Murray and Francis J. Rigney. Easiest book on the market, clearest instructions on making interesting, beautiful origami. Sail boats, cups, roosters, frogs that move legs, bonbon boxes, standing birds, etc. 40 projects; more than 275 diagrams and photographs. 94pp.
20713-7 Paperbound $1.00

TRICKS AND GAMES ON THE POOL TABLE, Fred Herrmann. 79 tricks and games— some solitaires, some for two or more players, some competitive games—to entertain you between formal games. Mystifying shots and throws, unusual caroms, tricks involving such props as cork, coins, a hat, etc. Formerly *Fun on the Pool Table*. 77 figures. 95pp.
21814-7 Paperbound $1.00

HAND SHADOWS TO BE THROWN UPON THE WALL: A SERIES OF NOVEL AND AMUSING FIGURES FORMED BY THE HAND, Henry Bursill. Delightful picturebook from great-grandfather's day shows how to make 18 different hand shadows: a bird that flies, duck that quacks, dog that wags his tail, camel, goose, deer, boy, turtle, etc. Only book of its sort. vi + 33pp. 6½ x 9¼. 21779-5 Paperbound $1.00

WHITTLING AND WOODCARVING, E. J. Tangerman. 18th printing of best book on market. "If you can cut a potato you can carve" toys and puzzles, chains, chessmen, caricatures, masks, frames, woodcut blocks, surface patterns, much more. Information on tools, woods, techniques. Also goes into serious wood sculpture from Middle Ages to present, East and West. 464 photos, figures. x + 293pp.
20965-2 Paperbound $2.00

HISTORY OF PHILOSOPHY, Julián Marias. Possibly the clearest, most easily followed, best planned, most useful one-volume history of philosophy on the market; neither skimpy nor overfull. Full details on system of every major philosopher and dozens of less important thinkers from pre-Socratics up to Existentialism and later. Strong on many European figures usually omitted. Has gone through dozens of editions in Europe. 1966 edition, translated by Stanley Appelbaum and Clarence Strowbridge. xviii + 505pp.
21739-6 Paperbound $2.75

YOGA: A SCIENTIFIC EVALUATION, Kovoor T. Behanan. Scientific but non-technical study of physiological results of yoga exercises; done under auspices of Yale U. Relations to Indian thought, to psychoanalysis, etc. 16 photos. xxiii + 270pp.
20505-3 Paperbound $2.50

Prices subject to change without notice.
Available at your book dealer or write for free catalogue to Dept. GI, Dover Publications, Inc., 180 Varick St., N. Y., N. Y. 10014. Dover publishes more than 150 books each year on science, elementary and advanced mathematics, biology, music, art, literary history, social sciences and other areas.